Lesson Study

D1210374

Lesson Study

Using Classroom Inquiry to Improve Teaching and Learning in Higher Education

Bill Cerbin

Foreword by Pat Hutchings

A Joint Publication with The National Teaching and Learning Forum

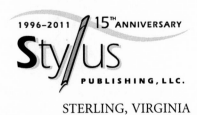

1996–2011 15ᵀᴴANNIVERSARY

PUBLISHING, LLC.

STERLING, VIRGINIA

Sty/us

COPYRIGHT © 2011 BY
STYLUS PUBLISHING, LLC.

Published by Stylus Publishing, LLC
22883 Quicksilver Drive
Sterling, Virginia 20166-2102

All rights reserved. No part of this book may be
reprinted or reproduced in any form or by any
electronic, mechanical or other means, now known or
hereafter invented, including photocopying, recording
and information storage and retrieval, without
permission in writing from the publisher.

Library of Congress Cataloging-in-Publication Data
Cerbin, Bill, 1949-
Lesson study : using classroom inquiry to improve
teaching and learning in higher education / Bill
Cerbin ; foreword by Pat Hutchings.—1st ed.
   p.   cm.
"A Joint Publication with the National Teaching and
Learning Forum."
Includes bibliographical references and index.
ISBN 978-1-57922-432-5 (cloth : alk. paper)
ISBN 978-1-57922-433-2 (pbk. : alk. paper)
ISBN 978-1-57922-721-0 (library networkable
e-edition)
ISBN 978-1-57922-722-7 (consumer e-edition)
1. College teaching—Methodology.   2. Effective
teaching.   I. National Teaching and Learning
Forum.   II. Title.
LB2331.C43   2011
378.1'25—dc22   2011012806

13-digit ISBN: 978-1-57922-432-5 (cloth)
13-digit ISBN: 978-1-57922-433-2 (paper)
13-digit ISBN: 978-1-57922-721-0 (library
networkable e-edition)
13-digit ISBN: 978-1-57922-722-7 (consumer
e-edition)

Printed in the United States of America

All first editions printed on acid-free paper
that meets the American National Standards Institute
Z39-48 Standard.

Bulk Purchases

Quantity discounts are available for
use in workshops and for staff
development.
Call 1-800-232-0223

First Edition, 2011

10   9   8   7   6   5   4   3   2   1

*Dedicated to my father
who was always there for all of us.*

Contents

Acknowledgments

I want to acknowledge the support of my home institution, the University of Wisconsin–La Crosse, and also the University of Wisconsin System Office of Professional and Instructional Development, which has made it possible to build and sustain the College Lesson Study Project, and through that project to support hundreds of instructors in their effort to improve their teaching and student learning.

I am indebted to two scholars, Catherine Lewis and Makoto Yoshida, whose work taught me most of what I know about lesson study. Catherine Lewis helped introduce Western educators to the practice of lesson study and her research continues to deepen our understanding of lesson study in both Japan and the United States. Makoto Yoshida's doctoral dissertation, *Lesson Study: A Case Study of a Japanese Approach to Improving Instruction Through School-Based Teacher Development*, sits on my bookshelf. It documents Japanese teachers engaged in a lesson study to explore first graders' understanding of subtraction with borrowing. It depicts lengthy, probing discussions about how young children understand subtraction, how they might interpret certain types of problems, what kind of errors they might make, and how to respond to them. Everything about the process and teachers' depth of understanding surprised and inspired me. This work has had a lasting influence on my belief in the importance of lesson study as a method for learning about teaching.

Finally, I want to acknowledge the patience of Linda and Flannery, who endured an unusually large number of blank looks and vacant stares while I worked on this book. It is good to be back.

Foreword

Not so long ago, the work that faculty did as teachers was largely invisible, undertaken behind classroom doors that were both literally and metaphorically closed, in what former Carnegie Foundation president Lee Shulman described as "pedagogical solitude." But that has changed. Today, faculty from a full range of fields and institutional types are finding ways to capture and share with one another what they know and do as teachers and to document and more deeply understand the experience of their students. Lesson study is part of this shift, and, for all the reasons described in this elegant new volume by William Cerbin, it is a particularly powerful one.

First, lesson study brings faculty together to exchange ideas and to collaborate on matters of instructional design and classroom practice in ways that make a difference. This sounds simple enough, but it isn't. I recall a workshop I led years ago—probably in the early 1990s—where faculty from the campus in question were invited to bring along and share a syllabus from one of their courses, walking one another through the design decisions embodied within it; along the way, it became clear that no one in the room had ever had the occasion to look closely at a colleague's syllabus. In lesson study, this circumstance is turned on its head and magnified, as colleagues sit together to hammer out goals for student learning and agree on a carefully structured set of steps for advancing those goals—and then, in an even rarer event, serve as observers for each other as the lesson unfolds in the classroom. This kind of close collaboration is not without its challenges; trust must be built, ground rules established. But as Cerbin's experience with groups in a growing number of settings makes clear, there are many faculty who are eager for this kind of experience, and grateful for the benefits that follow: close work with others who share their goals for students, a chance to see and examine alternative teaching approaches, and practice with new ways to capture the student learning experience.

Second, lesson study builds on the shift of focus from teaching to learning that has been under way in higher education for the past two decades.

The assessment movement comes to mind here, for instance, and many read-ers will know the landmark 1995 essay by Barr and Tagg calling for a para-digm shift from teaching to learning. What *Lesson Study* adds to the mix is a powerful reminder that knowing *what* (and even *how much*) students learn is not enough; in order to improve educational outcomes, teachers need to understand more about *how* students learn. In this spirit, my favorite phrase in the volume is "cognitive empathy," a term Cerbin coins to capture the importance of imagining how new ideas are experienced by novice learners. Doing so is pretty clearly an element of good teaching, but it is also a prodi-gious challenge; as experts in their field, faculty have often forgotten their own experience as onetime beginners, seeing their field's complex concepts and ways of thinking as a given. Thus, one needs not only an impulse to cognitive empathy, but a process for testing, complicating, and strengthening it—and that is one way of explaining the purpose of lesson study. Unlike some forms of education research, which aim for generalized knowledge about learning and teaching, lesson study stakes its claim on the ground, in the particulars of teaching this lesson to these students in this particular context. And unlike institutional and program assessment, which generates a more cumulative picture of effectiveness, lesson study looks not for proof but for understanding—and, one might add, for the next set of questions to explore.

In this sense, lesson study also reflects the growing shift to a more schol-arly view of teaching and a recognition of the complexity of pedagogical work. To put it differently, lesson study makes the otherwise mostly private domain of the classroom a site for systematic study and knowledge building. It does so not so much because teaching *deserves* to be seen as important intellectual work (which it clearly does), but because there's no alternative. Teachers who want to see more students succeed in more meaningful ways must attend closely to their experience as learners. Of course, it should be said, teachers have always paid attention to students' progress—assigning tasks, evaluating and grading those tasks, providing feedback—and many faculty revise their course designs based on what they have learned in a previ-ous iteration of the course. But *Lesson Study* takes this to another level, recog-nizing that getting an accurate sense of what and, especially, how students are learning key concepts, skills, and dispositions is no simple matter. After all, different students learn in different ways, start in different places, and bring different interests and motivations to the task at hand; and most are not eager to reveal what they do not understand (they have in fact sometimes been rewarded for going through the motions of understanding), though if they were, it would of course make this whole business of teaching much easier. With these challenges in view, *Lesson Study* calls on faculty to undertake what Cerbin describes as "deliberate practice," a necessary element, as research has shown, in developing expertise. More than casual observation and the trading of impressions (though that's valuable too and a good place to start), lesson study brings to teaching a process that is collaborative; structured; inquiry-oriented; and, yes, scholarly.

As these features of lesson study make clear, this is a volume about big ideas. But it is also a very practical resource. Readers wanting to put a toe in lesson study waters will find the guidance they need here. Drawing on the original Japanese model but firmly grounded in experience with faculty in this country, Cerbin sets forth a step-by-step model that is simple and clear. For those who have already waded in, or who are helping others to do so, the volume offers guiding principles; theoretical underpinnings; fresh thinking; detailed examples; and, more important, a window into the larger community that is now assembling itself around this important work.

I first met Bill Cerbin some 20 years ago. I was a senior staff member at the American Association for Higher Education (AAHE), directing a program aimed at helping campuses create a culture in which the work of teaching and learning would be talked about, inquired into, valued, and rewarded. It was a wonderful job that brought me into contact with faculty around the country who were doing wonderful things. One of those was Bill, who, knowing AAHE's interests, generously shared with me something he had created, which he called a *course portfolio*. Teaching portfolios were on the rise in those days as part of an effort to document pedagogical effectiveness for purposes of promotion and tenure. But the notion of documenting the teaching and learning within a single course was new and particularly resonant with emerging conceptions of the scholarship of teaching and learning. The rest, as they say, is history, as course portfolios have taken hold on many campuses across the country, been built into teaching improvement activities, collected in repositories, featured at disciplinary conferences, and written about.

I mention this little bit of history because it represents, for me, an important context for understanding lesson study—as part of a larger continuing tradition of inquiry and documentation but also as a further step toward concreteness and focus—moving, that is to say, from teaching in general, to the teaching of specific courses, to the teaching and learning of what Cerbin refers to as the "building blocks" of the course, an individual lesson. What's striking is that this tighter focus opens up all the largest questions: about disciplinary understanding, conceptions of student learning, the purposes of higher education, and the culture in which teaching and learning are undertaken.

My point here is that this is a book about not only lesson study, but about teaching and learning more broadly. A deceptively simple process, lesson study opens a wide door to a generous set of understandings and experiences. Cerbin has managed to make the process simple, in the best sense of that word. But his vision is a rich and ambitious one, important to all who care about the experience and learning of students in higher education today.

Pat Hutchings
Senior Associate
The Carnegie Foundation for the Advancement of Teaching

Preface

This book is about how to improve college teaching. It does not propose a new teaching method or advocate particular innovative teaching techniques currently in vogue. Instead, it focuses on the *process of improvement*, and explores how classroom teachers can improve their instruction using an approach called *lesson study*. In lesson study, several instructors jointly design, teach, study, and refine an individual class lesson. Throughout the process they explore student learning problems and goals, examine their teaching practices, observe how students learn, and analyze how their instruction affects student learning and thinking.

I first learned about lesson study in 1999 from *The Teaching Gap: Best Ideas From the World's Teachers for Improving Education in the Classroom*. The authors, James Stigler and James Hiebert, described how Japanese elementary school teachers carefully and systematically study teaching and learning in the context of individual class lessons. Almost all Japanese teachers engage in lesson studies each year, building and sharing pedagogical expertise. My first reactions to this were, "I want to do lesson study," and "This is what college teachers could be doing to improve their teaching."

At the time, I was doing research in my own psychology classes, investigating student learning and trying to use the results to improve my teaching. I wanted to know why students stumble over certain concepts and ideas— like why they attribute causality to correlation, why they have trouble understanding how the presence of other people influences individual behavior, and why they confuse negative reinforcement with punishment. Lesson study seemed to be particularly well-suited to investigating these types of persistent learning problems.

But it was not until I participated in lesson study that I began to understand the range and depth of the process. In 2003 a group of 16 instructors at the University of Wisconsin–La Crosse undertook a proof-of-concept project to try out lesson study in our classes (biology, economics, English, psychology). None of us had lesson study experience; we simply followed general guidelines of the Japanese model. It did not take long before we were immersed in something very different from other teaching improvement activities. I worked with three psychology colleagues. During our hour-long sessions each week we questioned our basic assumptions about teaching and thought about the essential goals of the psychology course, what students should really understand, and the learning problems students experience. We learned alternative ways to teach from one another, and co-designed new course materials. When I taught our research lesson my colleagues attended the class to observe and collect data about student learning. Afterward, they eagerly reported their observations; we analyzed and discussed how our lesson worked, how students had responded, what worked, what didn't, and what took us by surprise. We discussed ways to revise the lesson in light of the data. We completed two full cycles of the lesson study, and wrote and published our results.

By focusing on a single lesson we were able to examine every step of the teaching process from vision and goals, to instructional design, to implementation, to observation and analysis of student performance, and then evidence-based improvement.

That first experience solidified my belief that lesson study has enormous potential to help teachers improve their teaching and student learning. Since then I have promoted the use of lesson study among college instructors, giving many training sessions and workshop presentations. This book is an extension of that effort. It is the first book about lesson study in higher education. It is intended to introduce lesson study practices to college teachers and provide guidance and tools so that interested instructors can do lesson study in their own classes. It also explores lesson study practices in greater depth to provide practitioners with examples, models, and ideas about how to realize the full potential of lesson study to advance teaching and learning.

1

Introduction

Good college teachers are concerned first and foremost about whether their students learn what they are taught. We want students to achieve deep knowledge of the subjects we teach and develop the complex skills, sensibilities, and habits of mind that typify a well-educated person. As classroom teachers we can chart our successes and failures, our sense of efficacy, and sometimes our mood swings in terms of whether students make good sense of what we teach each day. It is particularly gratifying when students "get it," especially when they have been struggling to learn something complex and elusive. And, it is disappointing to do our best only to find that students don't understand the basic ideas we taught.

Learning in college is a formidable task. Every day, students confront large amounts of new, complex information. We ask them to absorb and make sense of it, and use it for a variety of purposes and reasons. But the volume of information is only part of the challenge. A more fundamental issue is that learning is inherently complicated. Certainly, students who apply themselves, try hard, and study can learn a lot; but teachers know that mistakes, misconceptions, superficial understanding, and underdeveloped skills are also normal consequences of the learning process.

To underscore its complexity, consider research findings on college science learning. Studies show that undergraduates enter college physics courses with serious misconceptions about physical phenomena. They may complete their college physics course successfully, but then revert back to their former misconceptions. For example, most students—including those who studied physics in high school—believe that an object that is tossed straight into the air continues to have a force propelling it upward. Yet, after it leaves the hand of the person who tosses it, there is no upward force acting on the object. Students relearn the concept of force in their college physics courses and do well on tests. However, at the end of their college physics courses 75% of the students revert back to their initial misconception that an upward force continues to act on the object (Clement, 1982).

Misconceptions and misinterpretations are common in every field. Even when students make a good-faith effort to learn, they often stumble, misconstrue, or otherwise fall short of where we think they should be. After reviewing the research literature on misconceptions and misunderstanding across disciplines, one researcher concluded:

> An ordinary degree of understanding is routinely missing in many, if not most students. It is reasonable to expect a college student to be able to apply in a new context a law of physics, or a proof in geometry, or a concept in history of which she just demonstrated mastery in her class. If when the circumstances of testing are slightly altered, the sought-after competence can no longer be documented, then understanding—in any reasonable sense of the term—has simply not been achieved. (Gardner, 1991, p. 6)

Despite our daily experience with students, we tend to know very little about how their learning takes place or how our teaching affects their learning. Our tests may reveal *what* students learn and don't learn, but not the basis of their performance. In class we witness moments of learning, for example, when students make insightful remarks about the topic at hand or ask interesting questions. At other times it seems as though students have only a vague idea what the topic is—or worse, they misconstrue it. But how often during these episodes do we know what led to their insights or misconceptions? How often can we explain what aspects of our teaching supported or impaired their understanding? I have walked out of class many times wondering *why* it went so well or so poorly.

To help us improve our practice we need to better understand how students learn, and attain more insight into the basis of their performance. We need ways to look inside the "black box" to see how students make sense of the subject matter and how our instruction supports or interferes with it.

This book is about how college faculty can better understand student learning and improve their teaching by studying individual class lessons. In this approach, known as lesson study, several instructors jointly plan, teach, observe, analyze, and refine a single class lesson. The purpose of a lesson study is to put a lesson under the microscope, to carefully analyze how students learn from our teaching and then use that knowledge to improve future performance—ours and theirs.

Why study lessons? Instructors try to improve their practice in a multitude of ways such as by updating their courses and materials, adopting new teaching practices, creating new assignments, and using alternative methods to evaluate students. But, why not improve teaching by examining the building blocks of our courses—class lessons? As teachers we devote a significant portion of our work lives to preparing and presenting lessons. Why not make lessons the object of study? As researcher Catherine Lewis (2002b) says,

> Lesson study is a simple idea. If you want to improve instruction, what could be more obvious than collaborating with fellow teachers to plan, observe, and reflect on lessons?

A lesson is the place where our instructional goals come to life, where students interact with the instructor, other students, and the subject matter. From a practical standpoint, lessons are ideal for study because they are manageable units of analysis. It is easier to investigate the teaching and learning in a single lesson than in a larger curricular unit or throughout an entire course. An individual lesson has fewer goals, less content, and takes place on a single day. By focusing on a single lesson, teachers can carefully and systematically examine how instructional activities play out and how students learn from the experience. What instructors learn from studying a single lesson may be applied more generally to other areas of teaching and learning. Moreover, changing a single lesson is less risky compared to adopting a new teaching strategy to use throughout an entire course.

Although they are small segments, lessons are complex units of teaching and learning. Consider what goes into a lesson. We imbue them with important goals for learning, intend them to shape student thinking, craft exercises and assignments to bring the goals to life, enact our plans in class, and reflect on how they turn out. By studying lessons—from goals to design to presentation to results—instructors can examine the entire teaching and learning process. Through lesson study instructors collectively can

- examine their goals for student learning;
- discuss student difficulties with the subject matter;
- explore how instructional strategies can support specific forms of learning;
- create a class lesson intended to bring learning goals to life;
- investigate how students learn or do not learn from the lesson;
- observe students as they react and respond to classroom instruction;
- analyze multiple sources of evidence about student learning;
- use evidence of student learning to revise teaching; and
- document their work so that other teachers can use it, learn from it, and build upon it.

In essence, a single lesson can encompass the full substance and complexity of teaching and learning—the world of teaching in a single grain of sand. And, by studying individual lessons teachers can develop deeper understanding of how students learn.

What does lesson study look like? Lesson study grew out of the collective efforts of classroom teachers in Asia to improve their teaching. It is particularly well developed in Japan, where it has been shaped by teachers and education specialists into a very powerful form of professional development and practitioner inquiry. The primary aims of lesson study are to improve the practice of those teachers who participate in it and to build knowledge that can be used by other teachers to improve their practice.

Because it has been molded by the needs and interests of practitioners, lesson study is different from more general models of educational research. You do not need an advanced degree to do lesson study; instead, you learn it by participating alongside experienced practitioners. Nevertheless, lesson study is not a casual, anything-goes procedure. It is a form of systematic inquiry that has well-established practices and processes.

Lesson study is a cyclical process that is broken down into a series of steps in which several instructors jointly plan, teach, and study a lesson. Figure 1 depicts the sequence of steps in the lesson study cycle. I describe them briefly in this chapter and discuss them more fully in subsequent chapters.

- *Formulate learning goals.* The first task in a lesson study is to define learning goals for a lesson. Typically, the lesson study team members select a topic of interest to them, usually one that is important in the discipline or course, one that poses problems for students, or one that is new to the curriculum. Ideally, a research lesson addresses immediate academic learning goals (e.g., understanding specific concepts and subject matter) and broad goals for development of intellectual abilities, habits of mind, and personal qualities.
- *Plan the lesson.* The team creates a lesson intended to "bring the goals to life" (Lewis, 2000). The teachers may modify an existing lesson or start anew. They share their previous experiences teaching the topic, and discuss possible ways to address the lesson goals.
- *Plan the study.* The team develops a plan to investigate how students learn from the lesson that specifies the type of evidence the team will collect and how observers will observe and record data during the lesson. Data typically consist of detailed observations of student activity and students' written work during the lesson.
- *Teach, observe, and gather evidence.* The lesson is taught at the scheduled time during the term. One member of the team teaches the lesson and other members, and any invited guests, attend the class to observe and collect data.

Figure 1   Lesson Study Cycle

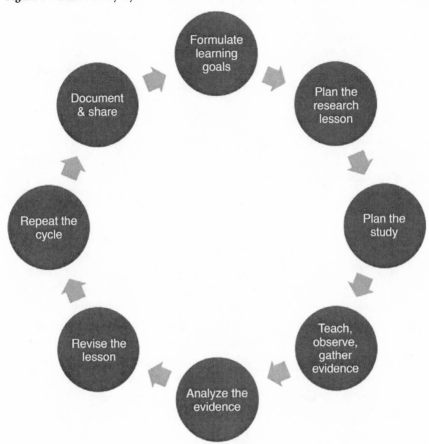

- *Analyze the evidence.* Soon after the lesson is taught the team holds a debriefing meeting to examine evidence related to the learning goals and to reflect on the experience. Participants include the lesson study team members and guest observers. Participants share their observations and examine additional evidence from the lesson, such as student written work, searching for patterns that may reveal important insights into teaching practice and student learning.
- *Revise the lesson.* Following the debriefing session, the lesson study team holds one or more meetings to analyze the data more fully and discuss possible changes to the lesson and/or the study. Based on the evidence, the team revises the lesson, which can involve anything from minor adjustments to wholesale revision of the lesson.

- *Repeat the cycle.* The team carries out a second iteration of the study, teaching the revised lesson in another class, usually the following term. Team members observe the revised lesson, collect new data, and hold a follow-up debriefing session to analyze and revise the lesson one last time. This iterative design process offers teachers a chance to explore ideas and different approaches, making evidence-based improvements as they go.
- *Document and share the lesson study.* Teams document and disseminate their lesson studies so that other instructors can review, learn from, and build upon their work. They produce a field-tested lesson plan accompanied by an explanation of the context and the results of the investigation.

To summarize, during a lesson study instructors examine learning goals and problems students experience in a specific class. They select goals or problems of special interest and then design instructional activities— exercises, lecture, materials—intended to support students' achievement. As they plan the lesson, instructors also decide how they will observe and gather evidence of student learning. Once the lesson and the data collection procedures are set, they take the lesson into the classroom, where one member of the team teaches the class while the others observe and collect data. The team then sifts through the data and decides how to improve the lesson. Typically, teams repeat the cycle by studying the revised lesson and making final changes. The team aggregates its learning, then documents and disseminates both the lesson and the study so that other teachers can use and build upon their work.

LESSON STUDY IN PRACTICE

Lesson study has evolved into the primary means of professional development among schoolteachers in Japan, where it is so pervasive that nearly all elementary and junior high school teachers participate in at least one lesson study during the school year (Fernandez & Yoshida, 2004; Lewis, 2005; Lewis & Tsuchida, 1998a; Wang-Iverson & Yoshida, 2005; Yoshida, 2005). Teachers also share their work in three ways:

1. Teams write lesson study reports, which are detailed accounts of the lesson and the teams' findings about student learning. These are disseminated widely in bookstores and other outlets. It is not unusual

for teachers in different parts of the country to know of one another's work.

2. Schools hold open houses—the equivalent of professional conferences—in which teachers from surrounding areas come to observe as school staff teach research lessons in their classes. Following the lessons, teachers hold a colloquium to discuss them.

3. Teachers publish their findings in educational journals. Japanese schoolteachers author thousands of articles annually (Fernandez & Yoshida, 2004).

Researchers contend that lesson study has been instrumental in helping to transform elementary-level teaching in Japan from a didactic approach based on drill and practice to a problem-based learning pedagogy, and has played a key role in elevating student achievement nationwide (Stigler & Hiebert, 1999).

These remarkable achievements prompt Western educators to wonder what kinds of cultural and educational conditions give rise to this system of teaching improvement, and whether lesson study can thrive in different cultural soil. College teachers may have even more pointed questions about whether educational practices used by Asian elementary school teachers are relevant and adaptable to American college classrooms.

Since Western educators first became aware of lesson study in the late 1990s, there have been numerous projects to introduce lesson study at the K–12 level in the United States. There continue to be thriving projects across the country and a growing research literature (e.g., Lewis, Perry, & Hurd, 2004; Lewis, Perry, Hurd, & O'Connell, 2006).

WHAT ABOUT LESSON STUDY IN HIGHER EDUCATION?

It is interesting to note that college teachers in Japan do not engage in lesson study, nor do college teachers anywhere else. Lesson study is by and large unknown in higher education.

Prior to 2003 there were only a few published accounts linking lesson study with university level teaching. Then in 2003, inspired by the Japanese model, instructors at the University of Wisconsin–La Crosse embarked on a proof-of-concept project to try out lesson study in their classes. As project coordinator, I recruited 16 instructors and formed four teams in Biology, Economics, English, and Psychology. We started with little formal knowledge of lesson study but agreed to follow the Japanese model. Each team developed learning goals, planned a research lesson to address the goals, taught, observed, analyzed, and refined the lesson. The following semester we did a second iteration by teaching and studying the revised lesson.

Faculty interest in lesson study spread quickly at UW–La Crosse and then to other campuses in the UW System. Between 2003 and 2010 the College Lesson Study Project (CLSP) has helped support more than 100 lesson studies involving more than 400 instructors in several dozen disciplines on campuses throughout the University of Wisconsin System.

The CLSP has demonstrated that college teachers can and will participate in lesson study. Using the Japanese approach as a model, it has adopted and adapted lesson study practices to the college level. The CLSP continues to train and support instructors to use lesson study as a way to improve teaching and learning. Although ideas about how to do lesson study continue to develop, we now have considerable experience with lesson study. Throughout this book, I will draw upon the experiences of college teachers who, with a modest amount of training and guidance, have carried out lesson studies in their classes. Their examples will help illustrate how college teachers actually do lesson study and what teachers can learn from the experience.

The aims of this book are to introduce college teachers to the theory, practice, and research on lesson study and to serve as a handbook for those who would like to learn to conduct lesson study in their classes. This book is organized around major lesson study practices—finding a focus for a lesson study, lesson design, how to study teaching and learning during a lesson, analyzing and using evidence to improve teaching and learning, and documenting lesson studies so that other teachers can use and build upon them.

Chapter 2 is a stand-alone lesson study primer that describes general lesson study processes and practices. Instructors can use this chapter as a blueprint or guideline to engage in basic lesson study.

Chapter 3 examines how instructors can form teams, select a course and topic as the context for a lesson study, and initiate a lesson study around important learning goals or student learning problems.

Chapter 4 explores unique features of planning a research lesson. There are important differences between everyday class preparation and designing a research lesson. Teachers employ a backward design process to first identify the goal of instruction and then design lesson activities to support it. Teachers plan a research lesson that makes student thinking open to observation and analysis.

Chapter 5 describes methods for observing student learning and thinking in the classroom and gathering other types of evidence. Lesson study focuses on *how* students learn, which makes observation an especially important source of evidence. This chapter explores the types of evidence of student learning you can collect and how to plan data collection procedures.

Chapter 6 focuses on different ways to organize and make sense of observational and written data. The goal of the analysis is to better understand how students learned or did not learn from the lesson and to use the data to improve future performance of students (evidence-based improvement).

Chapter 7 argues that a lesson study can make a valuable contribution to teaching in one's field if instructors document and disseminate their work effectively. A lesson study produces two tangible products: (a) a field-tested lesson and (b) a study that explains how students learn from the experience. Both can be valuable. Teachers can adapt the lesson to their own classes and circumstances and also learn from the study what to expect in terms of student performance.

Chapter 8 explores findings from the CLSP, and describes how college teachers have been using lesson study, what they learn from the experience, and how lesson study practices can improve teaching and learning.

Overview of the Lesson Study Process

While it may be a simple idea, lesson study is a complex process, supported by collaborative goal setting, careful data collection on student learning, and protocols that enable productive discussion of difficult issues. (Lewis, 2002)

If you want to try lesson study, where do you begin, and how do you proceed? This chapter describes lesson study processes and procedures in sufficient detail so that instructors can undertake the activities on their own. It provides general guidelines, highlights major choice points, describes practical considerations, and includes question prompts that can help instructors work productively.

As teachers we plan, teach, observe, and reflect on our class experiences daily. In lesson study, instructors do this in a more deliberate and systematic way. One way to understand the method is to think of it as a research cycle involving a sequence of overlapping phases and tasks. In each phase there is a primary task at hand such as developing learning goals, planning the lesson activities, or designing data collection procedures.

The major phases of the lesson study cycle are as follows:

1. finding a focus for the lesson study;
2. planning the research lesson;
3. planning the study;
4. teaching the lesson, observing, and gathering evidence;
5. debriefing, analyzing, and revising the lesson;
6. repeating the research cycle; and
7. documenting and disseminating lesson study findings.

PHASE 1: FIND A FOCUS FOR THE LESSON STUDY

The initial phase of lesson study involves identifying the course, the topic of the research lesson, and the "research questions" that motivate the study. Usually, instructors know in advance which course they intend to focus on but they do not always know what topic or problem to study. Initially, instructors should explore concepts or topics of special interest. These may be topics that are difficult for students to learn or for teachers to teach, new to the curriculum, or especially important in teachers' fields. Some teams approach lesson study with no specific learning goals or learning problems in mind. In these cases team members should discuss different course topics and problematic aspects of the course until they find a problem or topic of mutual interest to team members. There are two ways to focus a lesson study:

1. *Investigate a learning problem.* Investigate a topic that is difficult to teach and for students to learn in your course. Teams can identify several persistent problems in their courses and then decide which topic would be of greatest interest to study. For example, in the College Lesson Study Project a group of Earth scientists focused on well-known, persistent student misconceptions of geological phenomena. This approach appeals to instructors who are interested in better understanding why students persistently do not or can not learn particular subject matter.

2. *Investigate a learning goal or objective.* Study how a lesson supports student learning with respect to important course objectives. In this case, instructors design a lesson that addresses a course learning objective and carefully examine how students learn from the experience. Suppose, for example, that your course purports to advance students' ability to think critically. Instructors could design or revise a lesson to teach critical thinking and study how the lesson supports that goal.

PHASE 2: PLAN THE RESEARCH LESSON

In the planning phase, team members usually begin by sharing how they have taught the lesson, discussing and debating the merits of different types of class activities, assignments, exercises, etc. To keep the focus on student learning, though, teachers also pool their knowledge of how students in the past have learned or struggled to learn the topic at hand. Teams may create a completely new lesson from scratch, revise an existing one, or combine elements from several existing lessons. Chapter 4 will discuss the concept of a lesson and describe different forms of lessons.

- *Use backward design to plan the lesson.* Most college teachers prepare for class by organizing the subject matter into a form consistent with their typical mode of presentation. A teacher who lectures may prepare for class by organizing information, examples, graphics, and demonstrations into an exposition of the topic. A teacher who uses interactive strategies may create exercises for students to analyze, explain, debate, or evaluate the subject matter. In contrast, lesson study uses a backward design process to plan a lesson. Instructors start with the learning goal—what students should know and be able to do as a result of the lesson—and then propose teaching strategies that can support student achievement toward the learning goals.

- *Clarify the rationale for the lesson.* As instructors develop the parts of the lesson they should identify the reasons they believe the lesson will bring about the desired forms of learning and thinking in students (i.e., achieve the learning goal or overcome the learning problem). This calls for theorizing about how teaching affects students' learning and thinking. Discuss why the lesson should work and clarify how it will support student learning. To the extent possible, explain why the experiences and materials you have planned will support students' learning and thinking.

- *Practice cognitive empathy.* As teams plan the lesson instructors should try to take the perspective of a student. Imagine being a novice in the subject and what it would be like to encounter the subject matter and instructional activities. Try to anticipate or predict what might be difficult, confusing, and easy for students. Anticipate how they might interpret the subject matter and the instructional activities.

- *Design a lesson that makes student thinking visible.* Eventually the team will observe students when the lesson is taught. To the extent possible, design a lesson that makes student thinking open to observation and analysis. Even in large classes where much of the instruction involves lecture and instructor presentation, it is possible to include pedagogically sound activities that also bring student thinking out in the open. Chapter 4 will examine this design feature in detail.

- *Script the lesson.* Create a detailed outline of the lesson that includes the instructor's annotations and notes. The lesson should be described in enough detail so another teacher could use it. This does not mean that every word is scripted. However, the plan is more than a general outline and should describe fully the sequence of lesson activities, the material the teacher will use in class, the teacher's questions, and even possible responses to students' questions.

PHASE 3: PLAN THE STUDY

In this phase the team plans a strategy to study the lesson. This overlaps with the lesson design process, so that as the team develops the lesson plan it also identifies what types of evidence to collect and procedures for data collection.

Think of the study as an exploratory investigation of student learning during the lesson. It focuses on how students respond to the lesson, how they interpret the subject matter, which aspects of the lesson support or impede their learning, etc. Of course, a primary focus of the study is how students progress with respect to the learning goal(s) or learning problem.

To address these concerns, the team needs to develop a plan to collect evidence of student learning during the lesson. Some data may be in the form of student written work but it is essential to collect observations of students. The lesson is an enactment of the lesson design, and the best way to understand how students experience and respond to the lesson is "live observation."

- *Focus on how students learn.* A unique feature of lesson study is that it explores *how* students learn, not simply *what* they learn.
- *Determine strategies to observe student learning, thinking, and engagement.* Teams decide how and whom they intend to observe when the lesson is taught. The strategy should describe

  1. whom to observe (individuals, groups, entire class);
  2. what to observe; and
  3. how to record the data (e.g., detailed field notes of the entire class period; special attention to specific parts of the lesson; attention to specific aspects of student behavior, such as how many times they ask questions of one another).

- *Specify other forms of evidence.* Identify additional types of evidence such as written work completed during the lesson. This may include students' notes or responses to exercises, problems, or other prompts during the lesson.
- *Prepare observation guidelines.* Prepare guidelines that include a copy of the lesson plan plus student handouts as well as directions for observing the lesson. This makes it easier for team members or invited observers to collect useful information. For example, observers may be asked to record extensive, open-ended field notes or focus on specific students and aspects of behavior. The guidelines may also include focal questions that highlight key features of the lesson (e.g., To what

extent do students refer to evidence from the course readings during the lesson to support their positions?).

- *Decide whether to videotape or audiotape the lesson.* Video and audio recordings can augment live observation. However, do not use recordings as a substitute for live observation.
- *Consolidate and review the data collection procedures.* Prior to teaching the lesson teams should meet to go over their lesson plan and data collection procedures. Do a "read-through" in which the team reads the entire lesson plan and mentally rehearses the lesson. Stop as needed to clarify the instructional activities and data collection procedures. This is a final opportunity to rehearse how the lesson will take place and make any adjustments to the material or activities. It is equally important for the team to review how it will observe students and collect additional data.

PHASE 4: TEACH THE LESSON, OBSERVE, AND GATHER EVIDENCE

A research lesson is an integral part of a course, not a stand-alone event. The team presents its research lesson on the day it is scheduled to be taught during the term. One member of the group teaches the lesson, and other group members attend the class to observe and collect evidence of student learning, thinking, and engagement.

Prior to the lesson, teams should

- *Prepare the materials.*

  1. prepare copies of the handouts to be used in the lesson;
  2. schedule AV equipment and personnel (e.g., videographer);
  3. prepare copies of observation guidelines and brief the outside observers about the lesson;
  4. prepare copies of *Informed Consent Forms* and brief the students about the lesson; and
  5. schedule a time and place for a debriefing meeting to analyze the data and discuss the lesson.

- *Brief the observers prior to the lesson.* The read-through of the lesson should be sufficient to prepare team members for their roles and activities during the lesson. However, if you invite other colleagues to attend as outside observers, it is important to review the lesson and describe their role as observers. Traditional classroom observations tend to focus on what the teacher does during the class period. Observations of research lessons focus on students and what they do in response to instruction.

- *Brief students about what will take place on the day of the research lesson.* It is best to obtain informed consent from students prior to the class period when the lesson is taught. As part of informed consent you will describe the purpose of your study and indicate how student confidentiality will be maintained. It is also helpful to emphasize that the purpose is to better understand teaching and learning in your class and that you plan to use the information to improve the course.

  On the day of the lesson, be sure to introduce the observers to the class and describe what they will be doing. If you record the lesson (audio or video) be sure to reiterate the reasons for recording and how the information will be used.

- *Consider video and audio recording.* I advocate recording research lessons and the follow-up debriefing session as a way to further document and disseminate the lesson study. Recordings can supplement your written documentation most importantly by *showing* examples of student learning and key features of the lesson.

  Recording, however, presents technical challenges. Some teams do not have the resources available to record. And sometimes, actual recordings are of limited use because of video or audio difficulties. In addition, recordings should not be used as a substitute for live observation.

- *Teach the lesson.* Although teaching the research lesson is a special event, the team should take steps to reduce distractions and treat the class period like any other class period. Observers and the videographer should arrive early and set up in the room so that the instructor can begin the class period without distractions and delays.

  Students may initially be distracted by the presence of observers, but their presence does not automatically influence students' participation or overall lesson results. Students often report that after a few minutes they tend to ignore the classroom guests. We find that students are less likely to be distracted by observers if the instructor explains their role in the class period and the purpose of the observation.

  As the class period unfolds, the instructor presents the lesson while team members carry out their assigned observations. The team should decide before the class whether observers can assist in any specific ways during the lesson. Preferably, observers should not interact with students or become involved in an instructional role during the lesson.

PHASE 5: DEBRIEF, ANALYZE, AND REVISE THE LESSON

After the lesson is taught, the group and any outside observers meet to discuss and analyze it. It is best to hold the first debriefing session while the experience is still fresh, preferably within a day or two of when the lesson is taught. The purpose of this phase of the lesson study is to analyze and evaluate the lesson thoroughly and use the information to revise the lesson.

To complete this phase

- *Prepare for the debriefing session.*

    1. ask observers to bring their notes to the meeting;
    2. make copies of the lesson materials for participants;
    3. ask team members to bring additional questions to supplement those asked on the observation protocol; and
    4. bring summaries or examples of any written data collected during the lesson.

- *Conduct a debriefing session.* In the debriefing session instructors offer their observations, interpretations, and comments on the lesson. It is common to amass a lot of information during the meeting. It helps to designate a team member to take careful notes and to collect copies of any additional data from lesson observers at the debriefing session.

    Teams can adopt ground rules to make sure everyone has a chance to be heard. In the Japanese approach the instructor speaks first, followed by team members, and then outside observers. Teams may also choose to use a set of questions to prompt direct feedback first and then open discussion later in the session for additional observations.

    The discussion should focus on the lesson (not the teacher) and on analyzing what, how, and why students learned or did not learn from the experience. Participants focus on the basic research questions of the lesson study, such as how students progressed toward the learning goal and how the lesson supported their achievement. Or, if the lesson study focuses on a specific learning problem, the discussion should explore changes in student learning and thinking with respect to the difficult material. Usually instructors will want to discuss other issues as well. The content of the discussion should be guided by instructors' interests in what they observed. Inevitably, some aspects of the lesson will be unanticipated or even surprising. The debriefing is an opportunity to have a full and far-ranging discussion.

- *Schedule additional meetings to analyze the lesson.* It is unlikely that teams can fully analyze all their evidence in one session. Schedule additional meetings to examine written data and different aspects of the lesson as needed. Most often, the evidence consists of student work (e.g., written responses to a class exercise) and observations of students during the lesson. The group should try to use both to determine what students learned, how they learned it, and how the lesson can be changed to improve student learning.
To systematize their data, teams may

  1. develop rubrics to organize and analyze qualitative differences among students' responses and actions;
  2. focus on observations of pivotal moments in the lesson when changes in student thinking did or did not take place as anticipated;
  3. examine the entire sequence of lesson activities to determine how they contributed to student learning; and
  4. examine extremes in student performance, by comparing responses of students who struggled with the topic with responses of those who appeared to have little difficulty.

- *Propose revisions to improve the lesson.* The analyses should help the group identify possible revisions to the lesson. The first iteration of lesson study is not complete until the group revises the lesson. Because there is usually a lengthy gap between the first and second iteration of the lesson study, teams should document their revisions at the end of the first iteration of lesson study or risk not being able to remember what changes they want to make. A good way to do this is to annotate copies of the lesson materials, including the lesson plan, handouts, and exercises.

PHASE 6: REPEAT THE RESEARCH CYCLE

Lesson study involves a second research cycle in which the group teaches, observes, and further revises the lesson. In the first iteration of lesson study, analysis of the evidence leads the group to consider ways to improve the lesson. Groups may modify the learning goal(s), lesson design and change their strategies for collecting evidence. After deciding on revisions, the group reteaches the lesson. The second teaching usually takes place the following term.

The second iteration is an opportunity to refine data collection procedures. By the second iteration instructors may have a better idea about how students are likely to respond and may focus their attention on certain types of student behavior or parts of the lesson where changes in student thinking are anticipated.

FINAL PHASE: DOCUMENT AND DISSEMINATE YOUR LESSON STUDY FINDINGS

In the College Lesson Study Project, we ask teams to document their lesson study in a form that makes their lesson and the results of their study accessible to fellow teachers. The final report includes

1. a detailed copy of the lesson plan;
2. a description of the study;
3. an analysis and summary of the data collected;
4. reflections by team members about the key findings from the lesson study; and
5. supplementary materials, such as video clips of the lesson, observation protocols, and handouts.

Teams can contribute to the quality of teaching and learning in their fields by disseminating their lesson studies through presentations and publications. These may include

1. presentations to campus colleagues within and outside one's department or unit;
2. presentations at professional meetings and conferences; and
3. publications in professional periodicals.

SUMMARY OF THE LESSON STUDY CYCLE

Lesson study involves the careful design and study of teaching and learning in a single class session. It is motivated by instructors' sense of what students should learn (learning goals) or by what instructors have found is difficult for students to learn (learning problems). Instructors create activities and experiences intended to bring the goals to life or help resolve students' learning difficulties. They observe students and collect additional data about how students learn during the lesson. Based on the evidence, they revise the lesson to make it a more productive experience for students. After teaching and studying the revised lesson, the team documents its work in a form that allows fellow teachers to learn from and build upon their results.

Appendix 2.A:
Forming Effective Teams

ESTABLISHING GUIDELINES FOR WORKING TOGETHER

Groups that establish shared goals, work cohesively, and manage their time effectively are more likely to enjoy and benefit from the lesson study experience. Because collaboration is key to the success of lesson study, it is important to explore how groups are formed and the features that contribute to the effectiveness of group inquiry.

A lesson study group consists of several teachers (three to five) who are interested in working together to improve their teaching and student learning. Two people can do a lesson study but a group should involve at least three teachers in order to ensure multiple perspectives. There is no upper limit to the size of the team, but it is more difficult to arrange meetings and foster group cohesiveness with large groups. Based on observed difficulties of larger teams, I recommend a maximum of five or six instructors per team. If more than six instructors want to do lesson study form two teams that do separate lesson studies.

Team Composition

The composition of the team depends on the teaching interests, motives, and goals of instructors. Following are several examples of groups in the College Lesson Study Project (CLSP).

Discipline-based teams

The most common type of team is discipline-based, where participants are from the same discipline and often teach the same course. Introductory-level, multisection courses are an ideal context for lesson study. However, all the instructors on a team need not teach the course for which the research lesson is developed. Instructors from outside the course benefit from the process of goal setting, lesson design, observation, reflection, and revision even if the lesson is one they will never teach. Moreover, the team can benefit from members outside the course who can offer a fresh perspective on the subject matter or other aspects of teaching the topic.

Multidisciplinary teams

In multidisciplinary or team-taught classes lesson study can be a way to develop shared understanding of teaching and learning, and a way to develop a common experience for students. Typical examples are general education courses or first-year seminars that bring together instructors from across the disciplines. For example, a team in the CLSP consisted of instructors from the library and communication studies departments who developed a lesson on information literacy (Chilton, 2007). The lesson is taught by library faculty and is directly connected to learning goals in an oral communications course. Another multidisciplinary team involved instructors from different fields who all teach a freshman seminar (Bartell, Furlong, Gurung, Kersten, & Wilson-Doenges, 2007).

Multicampus teams

Cross-campus teams may also be possible if regular meetings, virtual or face-to-face, can be arranged. An example is a group of literature instructors from different campuses in the University of Wisconsin System (Chick, Hassel, & Haynie, 2009; Chick, Hassel, Haynie, Beck, & Kopp, 2007).

Teams with graduate teaching assistants and novice instructors

Lesson study is a powerful way for new teachers to learn how to teach. Lesson study can play a significant role in training graduate teaching assistants and novice instructors. In our project, there have been several teams with graduate teaching assistants, and many teams include newer, more novice instructors.

Teams that include undergraduate students

In certain cases instructors may want to include undergraduate students on their lesson study teams. Student time constraints can be prohibitive, but students bring a unique viewpoint to lesson study. Upper-level undergraduates, especially those with tutoring roles, may be particularly beneficial to a lesson study team. One campus in the UW System goes so far as to link lesson study with undergraduate research experiences. The students use the lesson study experience as the basis for their undergraduate research project. Student team members are sometimes able to pinpoint the types of problems other students will have in learning the subject matter.

BOX 2.1
Lesson Study Misconception

In a lesson study an instructor designs a lesson and asks colleagues to observe it in class, and then help the person improve his or her teaching. Lesson study is a collaborative activity; teachers collectively design, teach, and study a lesson.

Establish Ground Rules for Working as a Group

Instructors doing lesson study for the first time benefit from a basic orientation about the process. It is important to discuss the nature and scope of the commitment with prospective participants. They should know that the group will work over an extended period of time (usually two academic terms), coordinate multiple tasks, and meet deadlines (e.g., teach the lesson at a specific time in the term). The most productive lesson study teams adopt basic ground rules for meeting, keeping records, assigning responsibility for tasks, and moving the work forward. At the outset instructors should decide how they intend to coordinate their work.

Set a meeting schedule.

Decide on a regular time and place to meet. Teams usually meet six to seven times to prepare their research lesson, teach the lesson, and then several more times to analyze and revise the lesson. After the first iteration of the cycle teams usually do not meet again until the next academic term when they repeat the lesson study with the revised lesson.

Adopt a procedure for recording work.

Good ideas evaporate quickly. Teams lose time and ideas unless they keep a record of their work. Adopt a procedure to record discussions, decisions, and drafts of material. Document-sharing technology makes it easy to do this. Members can then make notes and additions on a shared document at and between meetings as needed.

Establish roles and responsibilities.

In most groups instructors share the responsibility for lesson study tasks. I advocate identifying one person to serve as a group leader/manager/coach to call meetings, keep the group on task, orchestrate the Institutional Review Board (IRB) proposal, and keep the group moving forward.

Learn how to do lesson study.

First-time participants are not familiar with lesson study practices. To make the most of the experience, teams should review basic processes and use the guidelines and prompts in this book to help members learn lesson study practices, incorporate lesson study materials into group discussions, and guide the overall work of the group.

Obtain human subjects' approval.

If you plan to present or publish the results of your lesson study, you should consult your campus Institutional Review Board for the Protection of Human Subjects. If you do need IRB approval, you will need to submit a proposal to the IRB. You will also need to ask students for informed consent, which describes the purpose of your study and how information from their class participation will be used for research purposes.

Teamwork Summary

Lesson study is a yearlong collaborative effort. To maximize your productivity and enjoyment, teams should adopt ground rules to manage their work. Establish a meeting schedule, elect a team leader if desirable, assign someone to record the group's work at each meeting, and plan ahead for human subjects' approval. Most important, engage in lesson study! Team members should familiarize themselves with lesson study practices. Use the lesson study prompts to facilitate team discussions. As you will see, many lesson study practices are familiar to college teachers. As teachers, we all plan for classes, teach, and reflect on our work—but lesson study structures these activities into systematic classroom inquiry and introduces elements that are different from everyday teaching practices.

Appendix 2.B:
Questions and Prompts to Guide Lesson Study

Teams can use these questions and prompts to guide initial lesson study meetings. They highlight the procedures, decisions, and tasks involved in lesson study. Bring a copy of this to team meetings!

FORM A TEAM AND ESTABLISH GUIDELINES FOR WORKING TOGETHER

- Recruit several colleagues to do lesson study. Ask prospective team members to read chapter 2.
- Discuss your interests and decide whether to do lesson study.
- Discuss why you want to do lesson study.
- Decide who will
  - call the team meetings;
  - keep meeting notes;
  - draft and update materials;
  - prepare the IRB application; and
  - prompt team members to learn about lesson study practices.

FIND A FOCUS

- Discuss topics, goals, and student learning problems of special interest to the group.
- What topic will your lesson focus on? Why did you choose this topic?
- What specific learning goals or learning problem will the lesson address?
- What long-term qualities will the lesson support? These are abilities, skills, dispositions, inclinations, sensibilities, values, etc. that you want students to develop in your course and program.

Write goals in terms of what students will know and be able to do as a result of the lesson.

PLAN THE RESEARCH LESSON

- Work backward using the learning goal as the starting point to plan the lesson.
- Propose instructional activities that will support student learning and attainment of the goal or help students overcome the learning problem.
- Practice looking at the lesson from the student's perspective (cognitive empathy).
- Propose activities that will make student thinking visible and open to observation.
- Develop a rationale for the lesson activities and sequence—explain how and why the lesson will produce the kind of thinking you expect students to achieve.
- Script the lesson—write a detailed lesson plan for the instructor to use and team members to follow.

PLAN THE STUDY

- What will count as evidence of student learning, thinking, and engagement during the lesson?
- In addition to observations of students what other evidence will you collect (e.g., student writing during the lesson)?
- Who will you observe (individuals, groups, entire class)?
- How will you record the data (e.g., detailed field notes of the entire class period; special attention to specific parts of the lesson; or special attention to specific aspects of student behavior, such as how many times they ask questions of one another)?
- Prepare observation guidelines in sufficient detail so that observers know how to carry out their observations.

DO A READ-THROUGH

After the lesson and data collection procedures are fully prepared, schedule a meeting to rehearse. Do a read-through of the lesson and the study, and make any last changes to the lesson and data collection procedures.

TEACH THE LESSON, OBSERVE, AND GATHER EVIDENCE OF LEARNING

Prior to the lesson

- prepare copies of the handouts to be used in the lesson,
- *prepare copies of the Informed Consent Forms* and brief students about the lesson,
- prepare copies of the observation guidelines and brief any outside observers about the lesson;
- schedule AV equipment and personnel (e.g., videographer); and
- schedule a time and place for a meeting to analyze evidence and discuss the lesson.

During the lesson

- observers should observe and not interact with students unless there is a pre-assigned role for observers (e.g., observers hand out material and clarify directions).

At the end of the lesson

- collect notes from observers.

DEBRIEF, ANALYZE, AND REVISE THE LESSON

- Try to meet within a day or two to debrief the lesson.
- Invite everyone who participated as an observer.
- Make copies of the lesson materials for participants and be sure observers bring their notes to the meeting.
- Bring summaries or examples of written data collected during the lesson.
- Clarify the purpose and ground rules of the debriefing before you start.
- Focus on the data collected and remind participants to focus on student learning, thinking, and engagement.
- Schedule additional team meetings as needed to more fully analyze the data.
- Divide responsibility for organizing and summarizing parts of the data.

Suggestions for organizing and analyzing data:

- Develop rubrics to organize and analyze qualitative differences among students' responses and actions.
- Focus on observations of pivotal moments in the lesson when changes in student thinking took place or did not occur as anticipated.
- Examine the entire sequence of lesson activities to determine how they contributed to student learning.
- Examine extremes in student performance, comparing responses of students who struggled with those who appeared to have little difficulty.

Revise the lesson:

- Rewrite or annotate the lesson plan, lesson materials, and data collection procedures. The revised lesson will be used in the second iteration of the lesson study.

REPEAT THE RESEARCH CYCLE (USUALLY TAKES PLACE THE FOLLOWING ACADEMIC TERM)

- Meet to review the revised lesson and data collection procedures.
- Meet to do a read-through of the revised lesson plan, lesson materials, and study procedures.
- Teach the revised lesson and gather evidence of student learning.
- Debrief and analyze the lesson a final time.
- Make final revisions to the lesson and study procedures.

DOCUMENT AND DISSEMINATE YOUR LESSON STUDY

- Produce a final copy of the lesson plan that incorporates final changes and includes all the materials used to teach the lesson handouts, such as assignments, slides, graphics, and instructor's notes.
- Produce a final copy of the study that includes

  1. a brief description of the course and the topic of the lesson study;
  2. the learning goal(s) or problem the lesson was intended to address; and

3. a summary of your results—what, how, and why students learned and did not learn from the lesson.

- Disseminate your lesson study:

  1. Present your work to campus colleagues within and outside your department or unit.
  2. Submit your lesson study report (i.e., the lesson study plan and the research summary) to the College Lesson Study Project Gallery.
  3. Submit your lesson study work for presentation at a professional conference and/or publication in an appropriate journal.

Getting Started and Finding a Focus

In the initial phase of a lesson study instructors select a course, a topic, and goals for their research lesson. This chapter describes the tasks, decisions, and issues instructors encounter as they establish the purpose of the lesson, what students should learn from it, and where it fits in the curriculum.

THE IMPETUS TO DO LESSON STUDY

In Japan, where lesson study is a highly developed form of teaching improvement, teachers collectively identify gaps and problems in student learning and development. Schools adopt a research theme that encompasses these perceived weaknesses. For example, in one public school the research focus was "for students to value friendship, develop their own perspectives and ways of thinking, and enjoy science" (Lewis, 2000).

The theme focuses attention on broad goals that teachers then try to address in their classes, and also use as a focal point for lesson study. They develop research lessons that address both specific academic content and the broader research focus, or as one researcher describes it, "make the goals come to life" (Lewis, 2000). The research focus is an overarching context that gives direction and purpose to teachers' lesson study work. Because it emerges from ongoing discussions among teachers about student learning, it represents collective problems that teachers observe in practice and want to solve (Fernandez & Yoshida, 2004). Moreover, those problems are not simple deficits in students' knowledge or skills but shortcomings or gaps in intellectual capacities and personal qualities. Thus, Japanese teachers come to lesson study with a strong interest in understanding and solving important learning problems.

What can provide the focus for college lesson studies? Many college instructors are drawn to lesson study simply to improve their teaching. Instructors see it as an opportunity to share ideas with fellow teachers. Teams usually form when one or two instructors become interested in lesson study and recruit a few colleagues to "give it a try." There is nothing wrong with doing lesson study for the general purpose of improving teaching and learning. Instructors can benefit from the experience without a clearly focused learning goal or a learning problem in mind.

BOX 3.1
Can You Lift 100kg?

Lesson study researcher Catherine Lewis documented a Japanese lesson study in which 5th-grade teachers developed a science lesson to introduce children to the science of levers. The lesson also addressed the school's research focus: "for students to value friendship, develop their own perspectives and ways of thinking, and enjoy science." The teachers created a lesson to develop children's understanding of levers in a way that also encouraged friendship, promoted independent thinking, and cultivated their enjoyment of science. To view excerpts of the lesson study see the video *Can You Lift 100kg?* at http://www.lessonresearch .net/PlanningCycle.html.

However, lesson study is a much more powerful tool for improvement when instructors deliberately investigate forms of learning and thinking that matter to them. And it is the focus on understanding how students learn that provides the best basis for improving teaching. So, beyond the personal motive to improve one's practice, why design and study lessons? What is the higher education equivalent of the Japanese school research theme? How do instructors get from general interest to focused inquiry?

Shulman (1998) observed that teaching begins with "a vision of the possible or an experience of the problematic." The "possible and the problematic" are two ways to motivate and give direction to a lesson study. One is to explore the possible—learning goals or outcomes. We want students to acquire certain knowledge, skills, and habits of mind as a result of studying in our classes and academic programs. Thus, lesson studies can be organized around important course or program goals. Instructors study the lesson in order to better understand how their teaching supports student attainment of the goal(s).

A second approach focuses on problems students experience learning the subject, or the flip side of this, problems instructors experience teaching the subject (experience of the problematic). Every teacher can identify concepts, ideas, or skills that are especially difficult for students, and these are fertile ground for lesson studies.

A LEARNING GOAL APPROACH: FOCUSING LESSON STUDY ON A VISION OF THE POSSIBLE

Lesson study can be linked to institutional, program, or course goals. A common approach is to focus on an important course goal. For example, a mathematics team might want to improve students' ability to interpret mathematics problems accurately. It is also possible to build lesson studies around institutional goals. A first-year seminar at the University of Wisconsin–Green Bay aspires to engage new students more fully in their learning. This is a broad goal not only of the course but also the institution, which initiated the seminars to help students make the transition to college learning (Bartell, Furlong, Gurung, Kersten, & Wilson-Doenges, 2007).

Why Learning Goals Are Important

A lesson is a goal-oriented activity intended to bring about certain types of learning, thinking, and behavior in students. The *learning goals* of a lesson are important for three reasons:

1. Learning goals represent the types or forms of learning that instructors value and view as most important in their courses and programs. Well-defined learning goals communicate expectations to students; for example, signaling where to direct their effort, what they should learn, and how they should engage the subject matter.
2. Learning goals anchor the lesson and influence decisions about what to teach and how to teach it. They form the backbone of the lesson, providing a clear focus for lesson design. As you plan a lesson, you need to consider how the proposed activities and experiences will support the lesson's goals and help students reach the desired outcomes. In this sense lesson study resembles *backward design*, the process of starting with the end point of instruction and working backward to determine how best to structure the lesson to support student learning (Tyler, 1949; Wiggins & McTighe, 2005).
3. Learning goals help you identify and define the types of evidence you will collect. Well-defined goals provide a blueprint of the types of learning and thinking you expect to see in the classroom. Without a clearly defined goal, team members would be unable to identify what

aspects of student behavior or learning are important and observers would have no idea what is important to watch for during a lesson. Well-defined goals point you to the types of evidence you will collect.

TYPES OF LEARNING GOALS

If asked to describe the point of a lesson, a college teacher will probably identify specific academic content or a skill that students should learn (e.g., knowledge of meiosis and mitosis in introductory biology). If asked to describe the point of a course or an entire program, teachers are likely to name broad goals related to intellectual capacities (e.g., critical thinking), habits of mind (e.g., changing one's opinion in response to new information or evidence), and personal qualities (e.g., curiosity or persistence in the face of difficult tasks). In lesson study teachers carefully plan not only a lesson that teaches a specific concept or skill but one that contributes to the development of important intellectual capacities and qualities. This means, for example, that a biology lesson intended to advance students' understanding of mitosis might also aim to develop students' scientific reasoning or cultivate their sense of curiosity about biological phenomena. An art lesson about different styles of painting might aim to cultivate students' enjoyment of the medium. A sociology lesson might try to promote students' ability to take others' perspectives in a lesson on poverty. Of course, complex abilities and habits of mind do not develop fully as a result of one lesson, but those qualities are not likely to develop very much unless we address them regularly in class. A single lesson can be a highly focused effort to address larger goals of your course or academic program.

It is relatively easy for teachers to identify immediate academic content and skills for individual lessons (e.g., a psychology lesson focuses on the concept of aggression; a mathematics lesson on the concept of a limit; an oral communication lesson on persuasion; an art history lesson on impressionism). More challenging is thinking about how individual lessons can address developmental goals involving complex skills, abilities, and values. Thus, in the early phase of goal formation instructors explore developmental goals that are of particular interest and importance to their academic program.

Some teams decide quickly on developmental goals. Others perform a broader search by looking at external sources. For example, some disciplines adopt outcomes for undergraduate education in their majors (e.g., Undergraduate Psychology Major Learning Goals and Outcomes, 2002), and at least one professional organization advocates a set of essential learning goals for undergraduate education (e.g., Association of American Colleges and Universities, Liberal Education, and America's Promise).

Another useful source for ideas about learning goals are taxonomies developed by educational researchers. The most widely known is *Taxonomy of Educational Objectives* (Bloom, Engelhart, Furst, Hill, & Krathwohl, 1956). Bloom's *Taxonomy*, as it is best known, delineates categories of objectives that encompass many forms of learning we try to promote in higher education. The complete taxonomy includes educational objectives for cognitive, affective, and psychomotor domains. Table 3.1 lists the objectives for the cognitive domain.

Another taxonomy that may be of interest to college teachers is presented in "Making Differences: A Table of Learning" (Shulman, 2002). This framework proposes that multiple abilities are likely involved in complex learning (see Table 3.2). Any of the goals can be viewed as an outcome or end point of learning. For example, the capacity to exercise judgment could be a primary goal of a course. But that capacity is not independent from other abilities; judgment may depend upon one's level of understanding of the topic. Or, developing expertise in one area may lead to gains in another. Performance and action could lead to deeper understanding of a topic.

Table 3.1   Taxonomy of Educational Objectives (Cognitive Domain)

Objective	Description
Knowledge	Exhibiting memory of previously learned materials by recalling facts, terms, basic concepts, and answers.
Comprehension	Demonstrating understanding of facts and ideas by organizing, comparing, translating, interpreting, giving descriptions, and stating main ideas.
Application	Using new knowledge. Solving problems to new situations by applying acquired knowledge, facts, techniques, and rules in a different way.
Analysis	Examining and breaking information into parts by identifying motives or causes. Making inferences and finding evidence to support generalizations.
Synthesis	Compiling information in a different way by combining elements in a new pattern or proposing alternative solutions.
Evaluation	Presenting and defending opinions by making judgments about information, validity of ideas, or quality of work based on a set of criteria.

Table 3.2   Table of Learning: A Taxonomy of Developmental Goals for Higher Education

Goal or Outcome	Description
Engagement and Motivation	Being involved, invested in learning.
Knowledge and Understanding	Recalling or restating information; interpreting and explaining ideas.
Performance and Action	Using knowledge in action.
Reflection and Critique	Using criteria to evaluate and assess.
Judgment and Design	Making decisions based on multiple considerations and applying skills under a variety of constraints.
Commitment and Identity	Internalizing values and showing development of character.

Reviewing these taxonomies may help you sort through the multitude of possibilities and reflect on the forms of learning and thinking that matter most in your field, in your course, and according to your own beliefs about the aims of higher education.

In the College Lesson Study Project, teams report that they have productive and substantive discussions about learning goals. Institutional and program goals sometimes exist as unexamined lists disconnected from courses and teaching practices. Some teams indicate that their lesson study is the first occasion in which they closely examine course, program, or institutional goals, and the connections among them. A biology team, for example, started thinking about goals for its research lesson, which led to a discussion about course goals and eventually to a discussion about how the course goals fit into the goals for the undergraduate major.

WRITING LEARNING GOALS

As teams decide which goal(s) to use as the basis of their lesson study they need to state them in a form that clearly specifies desired forms of student learning, thinking, and behavior. The accepted practice is to state goals in terms of what students should know, what they should be able to do, and how they should be affected or changed as a result of the lesson. Following are examples of learning goals that focus on specific knowledge and skills as well as broader intellectual capacities and dispositions:

- Students should be able to explain how marginality is linked to supply by examining diminishing returns and evaluating effect on marginal cost. (Economics)

- Students should be able to revise their drafts by identifying and evaluating main ideas. (English)
- Students should be able to analyze and explain human behavior in terms of multiple factors. (Psychology)
- Students should demonstrate reasonable skepticism and intellectual curiosity by asking questions about causes of behavior. (Psychology: From *Undergraduate Psychology Major Learning Goals and Outcomes: A Report March 2002*)
- Students should prepare to live with uncertainties and exasperating, even perilous, unfinished business, realizing that not all problems have solutions. (History: From Bradley Commission on History in Schools, 1995, p. 9)

Writing goals for a lesson study poses two challenges. First, developmental goals are complex and multifaceted, and instructors must decide which dimensions are most relevant to their topic and lesson. Suppose your goal is to develop students' understanding. Students can demonstrate understanding in various ways. A conventional way to evaluate understanding is to ask students to "explain" a topic. You can then judge the students' understanding based on the scope, depth, and quality of their explanations. An equally valid indicator of understanding may be the students' ability to use the subject matter to "predict" a future event. For example, if students were learning about theories, their ability to generate plausible predictions based on the theories would be a way to evaluate their understanding of the theories. It is not desirable or even feasible to address every aspect of understanding in a lesson. What is important is that you define the goal in a way that is consistent with your instructional activities and what you want students to get out of the lesson.

A second challenge is to define abstract learning goals in terms of observable behavior (also called *operationalizing* the goals). When you teach a research lesson, observers will look for evidence of student learning and thinking with respect to the goals. If you define the goals in terms of the forms of thinking and the specific content expected in the lesson, you provide observers with a clear idea of what to watch for (i.e., what evidence to collect).

Table 3.3 lists Shulman's developmental goals and includes behavioral indicators for each one. For example, if students are "engaged in learning" they might exhibit persistence in the face of difficulty, express interest or curiosity about the subject, or ask questions to clarify their understanding.

Table 3.3 Behavioral Indicators of Complex Learning Goals

Goal or Outcome	General Indicators or Evidence of Goal
Engagement	The student continues effort in the face of difficulty or confusion requests to know more about the subject expresses interest or curiosity spontaneously expresses excitement
Understanding	Quality of students' explanations of a concept Student's ability to use a concept appropriately in a novel context Student's ability to give an appropriate example of a concept Appropriate connections between student's new ideas
Skilled Action	The quality of performance as students carry out an activity or procedure
Critical Reflection	"metacognitive" statements, e.g., I don't see how these two parts fit together; We need more information before drawing any conclusions; I still don't get how this works Reflective comments made in individual writing Reflective comments made in group discussion
Judgment	Use of explicit criteria and standards to evaluate alternative views Integration of appropriate information as support for judgment
Commitment	Declarations to act in a specific way Makes a plan to follow a certain course of action Follows through with a certain course of action

It may take a few tries to formulate your goals in the most viable format, but this step is essential. Unless learning goals are expressed in terms of concrete actions, you will not be able to design instructional activities that target the goals. Moreover, you will not know what aspects of student behavior constitute evidence of their learning.

EXAMPLES OF COMPLEX LEARNING GOALS

To illustrate the process of goal formation, I will examine four complex goals relevant to higher education. These are intended to illustrate how broad, abstract, developmental goals can be defined concretely and brought down to the level of a single lesson.

> ### BOX 3.2
> ### Lesson Study Misconception
>
> *Teaching goals vs. learning goals.* As teachers we are accustomed to thinking about what we do in the classroom (e.g., I teach about *X*; I explain *Y*; I force students to think about *Z*). Our tendency is to think about teaching goals rather than learning goals. Sometimes teachers conflate the two and express learning goals in terms of what the instructor will do. Lesson study shifts our focus to what students do and what they will learn as a result of the lesson.

Example 1: Critical Thinking

If there is a universal goal in higher education it has to be critical thinking, which appears in university mission statements, general education goals, and course syllabi. Rarely do you see the concept defined clearly at any of these levels. How do you *operationalize* critical thinking, and move from the abstract label, *critical thinking*, to specific, concrete forms of critical thinking that you can identify, teach, and observe in a course and a class? One way to start is by defining critical thinking in different contexts. Think about what forms of complex thinking

- are important in your field;
- are especially important in the course;
- are expected of students on course assignments, tests, and class activities; and
- typify students as they enter the course.

The answers to these questions can help you formulate a definition that encompasses important discipline-based skills and is appropriate for the level of course and student. For example, by understanding *how* students think as they enter the course, you can identify what areas need strengthening. It can also help you decide what level of progress would be reasonable and realistic given students' entering abilities. It is also worthwhile to take stock of what kinds of thinking you expect of students on course assignments, tests, projects, and class activities. A quick appraisal provides baseline information about the types and extent of critical thinking in the class.

How one lesson study team defined critical thinking. I participated in a lesson study that focused on critical thinking in an introductory psychology course. Initially, we had difficulty narrowing the concept of critical thinking and decided to focus on *psychological reasoning*, the kind of causal thinking that psychologists do when they try to explain behavior. We asked ourselves what forms of thinking would be reasonable to expect and to teach in an introductory-level course. We discussed the types of thinking we hoped students would develop in the course and also the typical limitations we observed in student thinking. Our discussion went back and forth, proceeding by fits and starts as we tried to articulate our tacit beliefs about psychological reasoning. A turning point came when one team member suggested that students tend to oversimplify human actions and explain human behavior in terms of one major factor (e.g., students are likely to conclude that some complex act was caused by "low self-esteem" or "poor upbringing"). That observation helped the group recognize a difference between novice and expert thinking; students tend to see the causes of behavior in terms of one dominant factor while social scientists view the causes of behavior in terms of multiple factors. At that point our goal began to crystallize. Eventually, we decided that we wanted students *to be able to draw upon the subject matter of the course to analyze and explain human behavior in terms of multiple factors or variables.*

Our idea about the ability to think of human actions in terms of multiple factors is by no means a comprehensive model of critical thinking, but it is an important aspect of critical thinking in psychology. Moreover, by defining the goal as the *ability to analyze and explain behavior in terms of multiple factors*, we were able to develop instructional activities that make this activity visible and open to observations. We created exercises that depicted interactions between people and then asked students to use course material to explain the basis for the characters' behavior. They wrote and discussed their explanations, which allowed us to observe as they developed their ideas.

As you can see, our process was not a linear path that took us directly from the abstract concept of critical thinking to our concrete version of causal reasoning. I suspect this is typical of how teams formulate their learning goals. There is no recipe; instructors bring their own ideas and experience to the conversation and work toward goals of mutual interest. The process may include false starts, circling back, and detours as the group considers different goals of the course and even the academic program. Ultimately, what is most important is fidelity to a substantive goal for student learning that instructors think is worth investigating. An important by-product of these discussions is mutual or shared understanding of the learning goal.

This is an achievement in itself and can have long-term consequences for teaching. As instructors collectively analyze their goals for student learning, it increases the chances they will adopt a unified way to communicate expectations to students and evaluate their learning more consistently.

Example 2: Deep Understanding

All teachers want students to grasp the material and develop deep understanding of the subject matter in their fields. How do we move from the abstract to the concrete and forge a goal statement that allows us to observe *understanding* as it takes place? At the behavioral level, it is helpful to think of understanding as a mental or intellectual activity. This is where a bit of theorizing comes into play, and I will propose two models of understanding to illustrate how we can define a mental act in terms of observable behavior.

In the book *How We Think*, John Dewey (1910) proposed a model that views understanding as apprehending connections among ideas, concepts, objects, and events:

> To grasp the meaning of a thing, an event, or situation is to see it in its relations to other things; to note how it operates or functions, what consequences follow from it; what causes it, what uses it can be put to. In contrast, what we call the brute thing, the thing without meaning to us is something whose relations are not grasped. (pp. 137–138)

Dewey's idea of seeing relations as the basis of understanding provides a way to operationalize the intellectual activity in a form suitable for classroom study. The learning goal of understanding can be described as the ability to make connections among ideas and concepts. Instructors could qualify the goal further by describing the context and subject matter (e.g., *The ability to discern how concepts X, Y, and Z are related to one another and to explain the unique features of each concept*). *Connections* are made inside students' heads but can be externalized through instructional activities. For example, students may explain the connections among concepts, depict them using a concept map, or use a matrix to show specific ways concepts are related. In each case these activities can be observed by instructors.

Another model, proposed by Wiggins and McTighe (2005), defines understanding in terms of several abilities. They contend that people demonstrate "sophisticated insights and abilities" through the activities of explanation, interpretation, application, empathizing, and developing perspective and self-knowledge. For example, *explaining* is a process of restating concepts or ideas in one's own terms. A student's level of understanding is revealed to the extent that his or her explanation resembles the consensually held ideas about the topic.

This example highlights the difference between understanding as an end point or product of learning and understanding as a mental activity. As an intellectual product an explanation is what a person understands about a topic. In contrast, the act of explaining is a sense-making activity in which a person makes connections, interprets ideas, and puts together her own version of a topic: It is a mental act that reveals how a person understands something. In a lesson study we want to observe students during acts of understanding, as they try to make connections, interpret new information, and arrive at their own representation of the topic. Sure, we can also look at their actual final explanations, evaluate them, and determine how well or the extent to which they understand the topic. But in a lesson study, we want to understand how students arrive at their representation—how they put ideas together, what tripped them up, where misconceptions arise, how their preconceptions influence their interpretation, etc.

Here is an example from a lesson study team in psychology that highlights this distinction between understanding as a product versus a mental activity. The group defined understanding as students' ability to use concepts and material from the course to develop coherent explanations of a topic. During the lesson students engaged in several activities in which they explained different social behaviors. Instructors observed as students identified key ideas and noted how ideas are related to one another as well as how they monitored or corrected their grasp of the topic. In other words, instructors observed students in the act of understanding, *how* they were able to understand the subject. The team also collected students' written explanations and treated these products as *what* they had learned. They were able to distinguish qualitatively different types and levels of explanations (e.g., man-on-the-street explanations in which students produced unsubstantiated opinion and did not integrate course material into their explanation; well-developed explanations in which students successfully integrated relevant course material to produce a coherent representation of the topic).

Example 3: Empathy

Learning goals in higher education tend to emphasize knowledge and intellectual capacities. In addition to intellectual abilities, many teachers want students to develop personal qualities, sensibilities, habits of mind, dispositions, attitudes, and values. See Table 3.4 for examples.

BOX 3.3

Understanding as a Learning Goal in Higher Education

Many examples of student learning in this book focus on *understanding*. There are two reasons for this. First, understanding is a ubiquitous goal in higher education. We want students to probe below the surface and achieve more than rote learning. Second, there is consistent evidence that understanding is a hard-fought achievement and not an automatic consequence of instruction. Lack of understanding can be viewed as a ubiquitous problem in higher education (Bransford, Brown, & Cocking, 2005; Gardner, 1991; Willingham, 2009).

Understanding is a process in which a person uses what she already knows to *make sense* of new information. This happens as the individual apprehends connections among facts and ideas and combines them with her prior knowledge. Understanding is, in this sense, a constructive process; the person develops her own understanding or version of the subject matter.

Sense making involves any mental activities that engage students in interpreting new information and combining it with prior knowledge. *Explanation* is an example of a sense-making activity. When people try to explain a new idea, they articulate what they know, connect previously unconnected ideas, reorganize information, restate information in their own terms, identify gaps in their knowledge, and form a new mental representation of the idea. Explanation sets in motion attempts to make sense of the topic.

If deeper understanding is a goal in your lesson study, it can be helpful during lesson planning to ask one another how each learning activity in a lesson engages students in making sense of the subject matter. What is it about an exercise or task that induces and supports students to ascertain connections between new information and students' prior knowledge? Additional sense-making activities include predicting, summarizing, creating examples, analyzing, evaluating, synthesizing, combining, reorganizing, and applying knowledge to new problems (Carver, 2006; Schwartz & Bransford, 1998; Wiggins & McTighe, 2005).

Table 3.4   Personal Qualities, Habits of Mind, Dispositions

Personal Qualities	Habits of Mind	Dispositions
love of learning	empathy	attention to detail
open mindedness	tolerance for ambiguity	striving for clarity and precision
curiosity	creativity	ethical responsibility
inquisitiveness	persistence	civic responsibility
suspending judgment	mindfulness	adaptive expertise
informed skepticism	propensity to monitor one's thinking	willingness to make and learn from one's mistakes

These types of goals are often viewed as difficult to teach and to assess, which make them good candidates for lesson study. To illustrate, suppose empathy is a goal for an academic program and instructors want to explore how their teaching influences this quality. The lesson study team has to decide what empathy means in the context of its field, course, and lesson.

Unless instructors already have a working definition of empathy, the team should consult the research literature or fellow colleagues for advice about how to define the concept. In general, empathy is viewed as the ability to take the perspective of another person and to understand and experience the emotional state and reactions of the individual (Trout, 2009). Instructors might further decide whether their goal is for students to improve their *ability* or their *inclination* to respond empathically. The ability to respond empathically is a kind of capacity, in contrast to an inclination, which is a propensity or disposition to respond empathically.

By refining the goal and stating it in terms of student behavior, instructors can start to design instructional activities that support empathic responding and to determine what aspects of student behavior they plan to observe during the lesson. They create scenarios that depict people in different situations and ask students to write and then discuss what the characters feel or to predict their emotional reactions. The students' written responses and the discussions give instructors an opportunity to observe how they respond empathically to the scenarios.

Example 4: Adaptive Expertise

Adaptive expertise is the ability to use one's knowledge fluently and flexibly to solve new problems and sometimes invent new perspectives and procedures to solve problems.

Adaptive experts are able to approach new situations flexibly and to learn throughout their lifetimes. They not only use what they have learned, they are metacognitive and continually question their current levels of expertise and attempt to move beyond them. They don't simply attempt to do the same things more efficiently; they attempt to do things better. (Bransford et al., 2005)

Adaptive expertise encompasses a number of skills and dispositions such as metacognition (awareness and regulation of one's own thinking), monitoring of one's understanding and level of expertise, a desire and propensity to improve one's expertise, and the ability to use one's prior knowledge to understand and solve current problems. Because it is multifaceted, adaptive expertise seems unwieldy as a single learning goal. How can such a broad set of abilities be operationalized? One approach is to select an essential feature of the ability for study. For example, one element of adaptive expertise is *transfer of learning*, the ability to use what one already knows to interpret and understand new situations and problems.

This is an ability that resonates with college teachers. We hope that our students' learning lasts beyond the next test and the course, so that it informs their opinions in future situations; aids in making decisions; and provides ways to better understand people, ideas, and events. In the broadest sense, we want students to be able to think *with* the ideas they have learned and not simply think *about* them or simply remember them (Broudy, 1977). Transfer of learning is an ideal goal for lesson study because as extensive research literature shows, people often do not use what they have learned in new situations (Bransford & Schwartz, 1999). In practice, teachers are often surprised and disappointed when students fail to use well-learned knowledge in relevant situations. Transfer of learning is an essential part of adaptive expertise and can be the goal of a lesson study.

Transfer of learning can be framed as a learning goal in the following way: Students will be able to apply their knowledge of *X* to novel problems and circumstances. Instructors can create either a lesson that addresses transfer of learning as an explicit topic for the class or a lesson in which students are asked to apply previously learned information to new topics, issues, or problems.

In each of these four examples, it is possible to define a complex, abstract ability or disposition in terms of concrete actions that can be observed in the classroom. Although there is no formula for doing this, the key steps in the process are to develop a model of the ability or disposition and to define the ability in terms of both mental activity and behavior that can be observed in the classroom. These are summarized in Table 3.5.

Table 3.5 Examples of Important Learning Goals

Adopt a definition or model of the ability or disposition. Teams should examine relevant theory and research or consult with colleagues.	Define ability or disposition in terms of mental activity. What goes on inside a person's head when he engages in the ability or disposition?	Define ability or disposition in terms of behavior that can be observed in the classroom.
Critical thinking: purposeful and reflective judgment about what to believe or what to do.	Analyzes complex events in terms of multiple factors.	Uses relevant course concepts to explain behavior in terms of multiple factors.
Deep understanding: to grasp the meaning of a thing, an event, or a situation is to see it in its relations to other things; to note how it operates or functions, what consequences follow from it; what causes it, what uses it can be put to.	Makes connections among new ideas and topics.	Explains how concepts and ideas are related to one another; depicts graphically the connections among ideas and concepts.
Empathy: the ability to take the perspective of another person; able to experience the emotional state and reactions of another person.	Uses own experiences to speculate about how another person might experience or respond to an event; recalls the emotions one experiences in that type of situation.	Given scenarios involving social interactions the student describes what the protagonists might be thinking and feeling and predicts how they may respond to new information.
Adaptive expertise: the ability to use one's knowledge fluently and flexibly to solve new problems.	Uses previously learned knowledge to interpret or analyze a new situation or problem.	Given a new situation/problem, the person uses previously learned knowledge to interpret, analyze, solve, and make decisions.

Summary of the Learning Goals Approach

One way to focus and direct a lesson study is to investigate important learning goals. Learning goals are pedagogically important because they communicate to students what types of learning, thinking, and engaging are expected of them. They are important for instructors because they define the major point of the lesson and help to direct lesson design and planning. Learning goals are stated in terms of student behavior rather than the instructor's intent or actions. In lesson study, goals should focus on specific academic content as well as broader abilities, personal qualities, and habits of mind.

A LEARNING PROBLEM APPROACH: FOCUSING LESSON STUDY ON AN EXPERIENCE OF THE PROBLEMATIC

An alternative way to focus a lesson study is to explore persistent student learning problems in a course. The word *problem* simply means that students experience difficulty with some aspect of the subject matter. The problem could be difficulty understanding a particular concept or idea, or learning a certain skill. Problems may focus on discrete concepts or ideas (e.g., No matter how I teach it, students just don't understand concept *X*). Other problems involve weaknesses or shortcomings in student thinking or habits of mind. Both types are fertile ground for lesson study. Most instructors have no difficulty generating lists of types of student learning problems, and the idea of studying a nagging learning problem appeals to many instructors.

Instructors interested in a problem-oriented lesson study might review two areas of research on learning, both of which are accessible to college teachers across the disciplines. One is research on misconceptions and the second is threshold concepts.

Misconceptions and Preconceptions as Learning Problems

Misconceptions are a natural part of the learning process. As learners construct new knowledge, they may form misconceptions about the material. These are discrepancies between the learner's concept(s) and consensually held beliefs. Misconceptions are a common result of trying to make sense of new ideas. They can lead to further misconceptions and impede the development of new disciplinary knowledge. Research has shown that misconceptions are often difficult to change (Vosniadou, 2008).

When people try to make sense of a new idea they interpret the new information in terms of what they already know. During that process it is easy to combine the new idea with misinformation or attach it to the wrong idea or misconstrue it in some other way. In the broadest sense, our understanding is never all-or-none. Especially when concepts are complex and unfamiliar, we may have a good grasp of one part and a fragmented, superficial, or wrong view of other features.

In chapter 1, I cited a study of college physics learning in which students entered a course with misconceptions about physical phenomena. They corrected their misconception in the course but reverted back to their initial misunderstanding after the course ended. In every field of study and in every course, students enter with misconceptions and develop misconceptions that complicate and impede their learning. Misconceptions, stereotypes, and misguided beliefs create a challenging context for teaching. Lesson studies can be used to explore how students develop and revise their misconceptions. In some fields, especially the sciences, researchers have documented many of the most common and pervasive misconceptions (Gardner, 1991).

Threshold Concepts as Learning Problems

In every field of study and every course some concepts are more central and important than others. These tend to be *big ideas* that are pivotal in understanding essential ideas in a discipline. Threshold concepts may be considered "akin to passing through a portal" or a "conceptual gateway" that opens up "previously inaccessible way[s] of thinking about something" (Meyer & Land, 2003, p. 1).

Other authors have noted that threshold concepts are troublesome and complex ideas that may not be grasped easily or all at once. Given their centrality to the discipline, it seems that teachers would be interested in better understanding how and why these ideas are difficult for students to learn.

As you begin a lesson study, your motivation may be to learn as much as you can about your students and about teaching them. The process of discussing learning goals and student learning problems can lead you to think about who else might be interested in your study. Chances are good that if your students do not understand a particular concept, then students more generally may not "get it" either. Or, if you investigate a significant learning goal, it is likely that fellow teachers in your field will be interested in your results. Lesson studies can contribute to the quality of teaching and learning in your field by helping to shed light on the universal learning problems and important learning goals. Be sure to anticipate your work's broader audience.

Designing and Planning the Research Lesson

To be a teacher does not mean simply to affirm that such a thing is so, or to deliver a lecture, etc. No, to be a teacher in the right sense is to be a learner. Instruction begins when you, the teacher, learn from the learner, put yourself in his place so that you may understand what he understands and the way he understands it. (Kierkegaard, *The Point of View for My Work as an Author*, 1848)

As instructors select a topic and formulate learning goals, they turn their attention to planning a lesson and deciding what instructional activities will best bring those goals to life. By the end of the planning phase, the group will produce a *research lesson*[1] ready to be taught in the classroom. This chapter examines the process of designing a research lesson and distinguishes it from everyday class preparation.

WHAT IS A LESSON?

The term *lesson* is often thought of as a teaching and learning episode that takes place in a single class period or session.[2] But a lesson is not defined solely by a segment of time. A lesson has a point—a learning goal that instructional activities are organized and sequenced to achieve. In this sense, a lesson can be viewed as a conceptual unit of teaching. The day-to-day work of teaching is organized around planning and teaching individual class lessons that can take place in a regular classroom setting, in a laboratory, in a studio, in a large lecture hall, in a seminar room, in the field, or online.

---

[1] A lesson produced in a lesson study is called a *research lesson* or *study lesson*. The terminology emphasizes that the lesson is developed for the purpose of study, and not simply as a regular class lesson.

[2] In the online environment the time period of a lesson can vary. The term *module* may be the online equivalent of a class lesson. The key attribute is that a lesson or module is a discrete teaching/learning episode intended to support specific learning goals.

47

DESIGNING A LESSON

Few college teachers are trained in instructional design, and I suspect that learning to prepare for class tends to be an autodidactic experience. We figure it out on our own by taking into account our experience with different teaching practices, the physical setting of the class, the type of subject matter, and other factors (see Box 4.1). To illustrate, below is a description of how I prepared for class as a novice college teacher:

> In my first experience as a college teacher, I was concerned first and foremost with how to present the subject matter to students. I prepared for my introductory psychology class by using the course textbook as a framework. I viewed my role as transmitting knowledge to students and followed the organization of the textbook slavishly. I prepared for each class period by outlining the major concepts from the text and adding my own examples to illustrate some of the ideas. In class I retold the text, in my own words and with my own examples, and sometimes with longer explanations to fill in where I thought the text was incomplete.

Like many inexperienced teachers, I was most concerned about covering the subject matter. To me, a lesson was equivalent to a chunk of content that I explained to students. Perhaps the most glaring omission in this example is my lack of attention to student learning. I may have espoused learning goals for the students, but those were not a factor in the way I planned or taught the class; my primary concern was getting through the material.

Subject matter is important, and for that reason we want to make sure that students learn it. But if we truly want students to understand and learn the subject matter, teachers must become more mindful of the way that instruction supports or impedes student learning. The lesson design process is an opportunity to think about various ways to teach the topic and speculate about how these may affect student learning.

LESSON STUDY PUTS STUDENT LEARNING AT THE CENTER OF LESSON DESIGN

Instead of laying out the class period with content coverage as the primary objective, instructors select instructional activities intended to influence the way students learn the subject matter. They step back and examine their assumptions, beliefs, and theories about how students learn, and plan instruction that fosters the kind of learning they want students to achieve.

BOX 4.1
Factors That Influence How We Organize
and Teach Each Class Period

There are numerous factors that influence our choices when we organize and plan our classes.

Mode of instruction. Each mode of instruction (e.g., lecture, discussion, laboratory, studio, problem-based learning, experiential learning) provides a framework or schema for individual lessons. For example, traditional lectures are didactic episodes in which the instructor delivers information to students. Naturally, there are variations in this format. One instructor might lecture by first posing a problem or question and then using various perspectives to develop answers. A second instructor might simply pick up where she left off in the previous class and proceed by explaining concepts related to the lesson topic. A third instructor might start by explaining an idea and then use a classroom demonstration to highlight features of the concept. A fourth instructor might approach a lecture as a storytelling episode. Regardless of the specific approach, all are identifiable as lectures and distinguishable from other modes of instruction.

Disciplinary preferences for specific modes of instruction. In some fields, well-developed teaching traditions, or signature pedagogies, typify how instructors approach instruction (Gurung, Chick, & Haynie, 2009; Shulman, 2005). Signature pedagogies are most clearly defined in professional fields such as medicine and law, where clinical rounds and the study of case law, respectively, are central features of everyday learning experiences. For example, most classes in the physical and natural sciences include extensive laboratory instruction. In the arts, classes take place in studios and rooms where students participate as apprentices to learn the knowledge and skills of the discipline. In physical education, class may take place on the playing field.

Situational factors. The level of a course (e.g., freshman vs. senior), the prior experience and knowledge of students (e.g., majors in the field vs. nonmajors), the number of students in the class, and the physical design of classrooms (e.g., large lecture halls vs. seminar-style rooms) can influence the types and forms of instructional practices that teachers use. The introductory course in many disciplines is taught in a large lecture hall with over 100 students in the class. The number of students, the purpose of the class (survey), and the physical space

---

BOX 4.1 (Continued)

(more than 100 desks facing the podium) all dictate that each lesson will likely be a lecture.

Instructors' familiarity with different modes of teaching. Many college teachers have no pedagogical training and are likely to adopt the teaching practices to which they were exposed as students. Unless instructors deliberately explore alternative practices, they are likely to use a limited repertoire of methods and techniques.

Instructors' knowledge of student learning. Instructors' general and specific understanding of how students learn affects their day-to-day instruction. An instructor who knows that students struggle with a key concept is likely to plan a lesson differently from an instructor who is unaware of student learning (Cerbin, 2009b).

When you put student learning at the center of lesson design, you intentionally promote learning *by design*. In this sense, instruction does not merely create opportunities for students to learn; it becomes a causal factor in student learning. To illustrate, Table 4.1 contrasts two versions of a lecture. Version A is a typical lecture in which the instructor delivers content throughout the period, pausing occasionally to ask if students have questions.

Version A may be a solid presentation—a well-organized lecture with appropriate examples and illustrations to highlight the concepts—but version B goes further to support student learning. It covers the same content as A but attempts to elicit and respond to student thinking throughout the period. Instructor B uses students' prior knowledge of the topic to plan the lesson. Students test their understanding of the topic by writing their interpretations and comparing ideas with one another, and the instructor uses student examples to further analyze ideas and give feedback. At the end of the class, students reflect on what aspects of the material are still unclear, and the instructor then uses this information to plan the next class period.

Clearly, lecture A is not a good candidate for lesson study because there is so little access to student thinking during the class period. A lesson designed via lesson study will probably look more like lecture B, in which the instructor will anticipate students' prior knowledge and misconceptions,

Table 4.1   Two Versions of a Lecture

Version A: Standard Lecture Approach	Version B: Takes Student Learning Into Account
Instructor • gives a preview of the lecture—identifies the goals, major themes, concepts, and ideas • proceeds to describe and explain the subject matter throughout the class period • includes examples and uses graphics to illustrate points • pauses at three points during the period to invite questions • summarizes content at the end of the class period	Instructor • assesses students' prior knowledge of the topic and uses information to plan lesson • gives a preview of the lesson—identifies the goals, major themes, concepts, and ideas • presents a 20-minute lecture explaining different interpretations of the concepts • asks students to write their interpretation of the topic and compare their answers with a fellow student • collects written responses and then projects 3–4 examples to the class • leads a discussion in which students explain the responses • uses students' comments to highlight key aspects of the concepts • at the end of class directs students to write a *muddiest point response* describing what concepts are still unclear or difficult, and uses these responses in planning the next class period

try to externalize student thinking, and attempt to support and extend student learning of the content throughout the period. Lesson A is an opportunity for students to learn the subject matter; lesson B is an episode designed to engage students in thinking about the subject matter in specific ways.

The following examples illustrate lesson sequences that foreground student learning. I am not claiming that these are superior lessons or lesson structures, but in each case the focus on student learning is intentional; the lesson brings student thinking to the surface and makes it a visible part of the activity that can be observed and analyzed. These formats are deliberate attempts to cause or induce certain ways of interacting with the subject matter.

Writing/Discussion Based

1. Students complete an assignment designed by the instructor.
2. Before or at the beginning of class, students write responses to questions related to the learning goal.

3. In class, students debate their answers in pairs or small groups.
4. The teacher asks students to share responses, writing patterns on the board and asking strategic questions.
5. Students revise their written answers in light of group discussion.

Problem/Case Based

1. The instructor presents a problem (or case, question, task, issue, etc.) to the class.
2. Students work in groups to propose solutions and discuss how they arrived at them.
3. The instructor provides an overview of solution strategies.
4. Students attempt to solve a new problem alone or in groups, and then discuss their solution strategies.
5. The instructor leads a summary discussion of solution strategies.

Online/Hybrid Based

1. Before class, students visit selected websites and participate in an online discussion forum.
2. The instructor responds to student discussions in an audio recording, which is then uploaded as a podcast.
3. Students listen to the instructor's podcast and then post responses to several focused questions.
4. In an online or a face-to-face class meeting, the instructor responds to selected student posts or highlights patterns in the posts.
5. The entire session is archived on the course website.

Typical Japanese Lesson

It is common in Japan for elementary and junior high school lessons to follow the pattern below. This form is so well-defined that each part of the lesson has a distinct name and specific instructional purpose:

1. *hatsumon*—presentation of a problem to stimulate students' thinking
2. *shu hatsuman*—the main assignment or problem to solve
3. *neriage*—sharing and refining solution strategies
4. *matome*—wrapping up, summarizing

DESIGNING A RESEARCH LESSON: WHAT MAKES LESSON STUDY DIFFERENT FROM EVERYDAY CLASS PREPARATION?

Although I use the terms *planning* and *design* interchangeably, each emphasizes different activities. Planning includes doing much of the practical preparation, such as assembling materials and getting things ready for the class. The term *design* implies conceptual work, in which instructors examine various instructional strategies and activities and discuss how these can address the lesson's goals. Instructors also decide how to sequence the activities to best achieve their aim. The design is intended to bring about the kinds of learning and thinking embodied in the goals. The lesson is put together a certain way to achieve those ends. *Design* also suggests that there is a causal connection between instruction and learning. In lesson study there are five significant features of the design process, which are discussed next.

Collaborative Design

Teachers jointly design the lesson. Typically this means that team members share how they have taught the topic and addressed the learning goal, or how they would go about doing so. They discuss the merits of different types of class activities, assignments, exercises, etc. They also pool their knowledge about how students have learned or struggled to learn the topic. For many instructors, lesson study is their first experience in co-designing a class lesson. Teachers discover new ideas from one another and are often surprised at the variety and depth of experience in the group. In the College Lesson Study Project (CLSP), participants cite collaboration and peer interaction as especially important and gratifying aspects of the lesson study experience.

Backward Design

In *backward design*, instructors first specify learning goals or outcomes of a lesson and then choose content and instructional activities intended to support those goals. This is called *backward design* because it reverses the typical planning process of using the subject matter as the starting point and organizational focus to plan the lesson. Learning goals not only give purpose and direction to the lesson, but also change the nature of the design process. As they discuss various teaching practices, instructors must think through how each one supports the lesson's goals (Tyler, 1949; Wiggins & McTighe, 2005). Instructors try to forecast how the instructional strategies will support student thinking and undergird their attempts to make sense of the subject matter.

Sometimes, instructors neglect to use a backward design perspective as they design their research lessons; this may be a result of failing to think through how students might respond to instruction or how the strategies actually promote, support, and scaffold student thinking. However, instructors often report that after participating in lesson study, they focus more on student learning goals in their everyday class preparation—thinking about the lesson in terms of what students should learn, and not solely in terms of what subject matter should be taught.

Making Student Thinking Visible

Instructors intentionally design a lesson that makes student learning and thinking open to observation and analysis, especially the thinking relevant to the learning goal(s) of the lesson or to the specific learning problem under investigation.

There is nothing unique or new about externalizing student thinking; it commonly occurs in classes when students respond in writing, discuss in small groups, answer questions, and ask questions about the topic at hand. In lesson study, however, the attempt to bring thinking to the surface is more deliberate. Of course, making student thinking visible is more challenging in large-enrollment classes where the main mode of instruction is lecture or when opportunities for student interaction are limited. Yet, even large, lecture-oriented classes can include active learning strategies that engage students in pedagogically meaningful activities that make their thinking open to observation. Some examples are included at the end of this chapter.

When instructors participate in lesson study, they sometimes alter the way they would ordinarily teach a topic as they try to design activities that make student thinking visible. The challenge is not simply to externalize student thinking, but to do so in a way that is pedagogically meaningful and that supports the lesson's goals.

Cognitive Empathy

Accomplished lesson study practitioners try to imagine what it would be like to encounter the lesson from a student's perspective. I call this form of perspective-taking *cognitive empathy* because it involves looking at the subject matter and the instructional activities from a student's point of view, trying to understand what it would be like to experience the lesson as a novice (cited in Hammerness, Darling-Hammond, & Shulman, 2002).

BOX 4.2
Lesson Study Misconception

You can't make thinking visible. Teachers sometimes reject the idea that it is possible to make thinking visible. Consider two examples from the cognitive sciences in which students reveal their thinking as they work on specific tasks.

Understanding physical laws. Researchers gain access to students' physics concepts and theories by observing how students solve problems and how they explain their answers. They have documented a wide range of students' preconceptions and misconceptions of physics concepts (Clement, 1982). For example, many college students believe that an object tossed into the air—such as a coin—has a force acting on it that pushes it upward. However, the sole force acting on the coin *in flight* is the force of gravity. This and other misconceptions are not only pervasive but persistent. Students who successfully complete a college physics course where they learn about *forces* often revert back to their prior misconceptions after the course. See Appendix 4.B for an example of how a teacher can use ConcepTests to discern students' conceptual understanding in the classroom.

Historical thinking. Think aloud is a procedure in which a person says out loud what he or she is thinking while working on a task. It is not an after-the-fact account by the person of what he or she thought, but rather a *streaming* narration of what the person is thinking throughout the task. Researcher Sam Wineburg uses think alouds to investigate historical thinking, in which college students and professional historians think aloud as they read and interpret historical documents. His studies reveal important differences between novices and experts in how they make sense of historical texts. For instance, professional historians start by asking questions about the author—who the person was, why the person wrote the piece—in an attempt to establish a context for interpreting the document. Novices, in contrast, pay no attention to the author. They read the document and try to understand the text (Wineburg, 2001). See Appendix 4.B for an example of how to modify these techniques for classroom use.

As they design a research lesson, Japanese teachers predict how students will perceive, interpret, and construe the subject matter and the lesson activities. This enables them to plan instruction that is specific to the way students construe the material. Moreover, in the planning process they go a step further by anticipating how they will respond to student questions or difficulties. Their predictions and potential responses are actually a part of their written lesson plan—that is, they specify what they will do in teaching the lesson, how their students are likely to respond to it, and how they will in turn respond to their students.

College teachers vary in their ability to predict how instruction will affect student thinking. Ostensibly, teachers who regularly observe their students interacting with the subject matter (e.g., writing and mathematics teachers) may be more familiar with student thinking than other instructors. Most of us catch glimpses of student thinking during our classes when students ask or answer questions, but we still may not have enough "data" to assemble the students' views. Moreover, college teachers sometimes overlook the large gap between their own understanding of the subject matter and that of their students—sometimes called the *expert blind spot* (Nathan & Petrosino, 2003). Over time, we become so familiar with our subject matter that our understanding of it becomes automatic, a given. We lose sight of the fact that for each new group of students, the content is new and unfamiliar. It may become more difficult to put aside what we know and to think like a novice. Japanese teachers become adept at gauging student thinking because of their ongoing experiences observing research lessons and engaging in lesson study. Imagine the cumulative effect of observing dozens of class lessons. (See Appendix 4.A for a sample college lesson plan with predictions of student responses.)

Identifying How the Instructional Activities Affect Student Learning

Lesson design involves a bit of theorizing in which instructors develop explanations about how the instructional activities will affect student learning. Think of the explanation as a kind of causal analysis or a model to explain how the instructional activities will scaffold or induce certain types of learning and thinking. For example, if instructors use a small-group exercise during a class, then they should try to explain how the exercise will produce the desired form of student thinking.

Knowing how students learn what we teach them is exactly the kind of information we need in order to improve our instruction (Cerbin, 2009a). For example, knowing *how* students misconstrue a key concept may help us

---

BOX 4.3
Predicting How Students Will Respond to Teaching

In Japanese lesson studies, teachers devote considerable time to mulling over how various elements of a research lesson will affect student learning and thinking. Their written research lesson plans include detailed predictions about how students will respond mentally to different parts of the lesson. Yoshida (1999) observed a lesson study in which teachers developed a first grade arithmetic lesson that introduced the concept of *borrowing* in subtraction. Teachers debated extensively about which two numbers to use in their initial subtraction problem to illustrate regrouping. This might appear to be an odd discussion—why spend time deciding whether $12 - 7$ is better than $12 - 9$ or $13 - 9$? They did this out of concern about what misconceptions and mistakes students might make for each problem and what students could learn from them. These teachers had an acute awareness of what their students already understood about mathematics, how they would interpret the arithmetic problems, and what kinds of difficulties the new concepts would pose for them.

---

devise different examples, explanations, or exercises that resolve the misconception and develop a better understanding of the concept. The acts of predicting, explaining, and theorizing during lesson planning can help instructors deepen their own knowledge of how teaching affects learning. When the team teaches the research lesson, instructors then have an opportunity to test out and refine their models.

AN EXAMPLE OF LESSON DESIGN: PUTTING IT ALL TOGETHER

To illustrate the lesson design process, consider an example from a large introductory course in which instructors decide to investigate why students do not understand a particular concept. Team members are aware they need to consider ways to make student thinking visible in a class that is typically dominated by teacher presentations and where opportunities for student interaction are limited. As they discuss different approaches to teaching the concept, they also speculate about why students find the concept trouble-some (*cognitive empathy*). Their ideas about this differ, so part of their objec-tive during the research lesson is to get better "data" about how students actually interpret the idea. At the heart of the lesson are multiple opportuni-ties for students to make their understanding explicit and then revise their conceptions. The instructional sequence includes a short lecture and several activities to induce changes in student thinking (*backward design*). Table 4.2 identifies each part of the lesson and indicates how it is intended to foster student learning and thinking.

This instructional sequence supports the development of students' under-standing and also gains access to their thinking at several points during the lesson: At the beginning of class, when students articulate their initial under-standing; after the lecture, when each student has a chance to explain and compare his or her ideas with another student; after the demonstration, when they have an opportunity to confirm or revise their understanding again when the instructor uses student examples to highlight key features of the material; and at the end of class, when students reflect on changes in their thinking. The instructors speculate that multiple encounters with the topic will help students become aware of their own understanding, and that new information and feedback will help the instructors to revise and extend their representation of the topic (*identifying how the lesson affects student thinking*). This example illustrates the use of pedagogically sound strategies to promote student learn-ing and make student thinking visible in large classes. In this case, students produce both written and oral evidence of their understanding. Note that student thinking is visible at four points during the class period.

What about the rationale or explanation for the lesson? How do the proposed lesson activities affect students' thinking? Table 4.2 identifies each part of the lesson and indicates how it is intended to foster student learning and thinking. Overall, the lesson engages students in predicting, explaining, and reflecting on how their understanding changes during the class period. At several points they receive feedback from fellow students and the instruc-tor, which they can then use to adjust their thinking.

Instructors often have difficulty theorizing about how instruction affects learning until after they have studied the lesson and observed how students react to it. To help you think about the causal nature of instruction, Appen-dix 4.B provides several examples of specific teaching techniques and exam-ples of how they will likely influence student learning and thinking.

PREPARING THE LESSON FOR CLASS

Lesson study teams vary in terms of how much time they spend in lesson planning, but most teams complete the research lesson in four to six

Table 4.2 How Each Segment of a Lesson Affects Student Thinking

	Lesson Activity	How Instruction Affects Student Thinking	Is Student Thinking Observable?
1	Instructor asks students to write an explanation or interpretation of the concept.	When students articulate their initial understanding, they create connections among ideas.	Yes: written responses
2	Instructor presents a 15-minute lecture.	Students have access to a coherent version of the concept.	No
3	Instructor prepares students for a classroom demonstration and asks them to predict and explain the outcome in writing.	Based on their current understanding, students speculate how the concept will work in a real situation.	Yes: written prediction and explanation
4	Instructor asks students to compare and discuss answers with classmates. Instructor collects responses.	Students organize and state ideas in their own words. Exchange of ideas is feedback students can use to identify gaps in their understanding and different ways to interpret the concept.	Yes: student discussions
5	Instructor reads several student predictions and explanations and then carries out the demonstration.	Students compare their predictions to the actual outcome.	Yes: if students interact during the discussion
6	Instructor explains the outcome and asks students to compare it to their prediction and explanation.	Students use instructor's explanation as feedback to revise their understanding.	No
7	Instructor summarizes key ideas from the class period.	Students have access to key points and essential features of the concept.	No
8	At the end of class, students compare their initial and end-of-class explanations of the concept; describe changes in understanding; and highlight gaps, misconceptions, and aspects of the concept still not well-understood.	Students look for changes in their understanding and identify remaining questions and gaps in their model.	Yes: final written responses

meetings. The lesson itself should be written out in detail—think of it as scripted—so that during the lesson, the instructor, other team members, and observers know exactly what the instructor will do and say, and what students will do. Additionally, the team must prepare other lesson materials such as handouts, slides, and graphics.

Appendix 4.A:
An Example of a Brief College Lesson Plan and Predicted Student Responses

CONSTRUCT VALIDITY LESSON PLAN

Step 1: 10 minutes

- Break students into groups and distribute group worksheets (direct students to introduce themselves to group members).
- Describe basic task:
  - Students will create "mini" tests of depression (as they define it) and propose research studies to determine if their tests accurately measure depression.
- Give additional directions.
  - Take individual notes so that you have the information (you will be handing in the group worksheet)—accommodations for the "recorder."
  - Be sure everyone reads his or her definition out loud.
  - Your group definition does not have to be the "perfect" definition, given time limit.
  - You will have about 10 minutes to complete this step.

Step 2: 10 minutes

- Instruct groups to finish definitions and begin writing items.
- Items should be related to their definitions/essential characteristics of a depressed person.
- Review Likert scale anchors.
- Remind them to spend about 10 minutes to complete this step.

Step 3: **30 to 40 minutes**

- Instruct groups to finish writing items and begin to propose research studies to determine if their tests actually measure depression.
  - Remind them:
    - There are unlimited resources—funding, people from a variety of settings (e.g., clinics, university, whatever), ages, diagnoses.
    - Think about your definitions of depression, what you know about depression as you think about what results you might expect.
- Monitor group progress; if groups seem to be going well, let them continue.
- If groups are struggling or off track, call to groups' attention.
- Pick some examples to review.

Step 4: **15 minutes**

- Call for attention and provide instructions for final method.
- Distribute additional measures.
- Think about how you might use these tests to provide evidence of the ability of your test to measure depression well.
  - Hint: Think about the statistical methods we have covered in class to this point.

Step 5: **10 minutes**

- After all groups have completed the task, if time, discuss some of the definitions and methods.
- Have group members describe as worksheets are displayed on visualizer.
- Save 5 minutes at end (if possible) for a writing exercise:
  - What was the most difficult part of this exercise?
  - What was the most important thing you learned from today's lesson?
  - What is still confusing?

PREDICTED STUDENT RESPONSES

Students will work in small groups to develop a paper-and-pencil test of depression and determine ways to evaluate the construct validity of their test.

Major steps in the lesson:

1. Students read their individual definitions of depression and use them to develop a group definition.
   - Expect students to share their definitions and combine or integrate ideas into a group definition.
   - Note that definitions may not be sophisticated or comprehensive given the short time period (10 minutes).
   - Ask yourself, Do the students recognize they have invented a construct?
2. Based on their definition, each group creates test items to measure the characteristics of depression.
   - Students develop Likert scale items. It may be challenging to form good questions in this format.
3. The group proposes research studies to determine the validity of their test. (This is the most difficult part of the lesson.) Students must examine the logic of construct validity studies to propose an appropriate study.
   - Students must connect their prior understanding of validity studies to their test of depression.
   - Anticipate that some groups will not understand the logic behind the validity studies. The instructor will monitor groups and intervene if they are struggling. It may be necessary for the instructor to address the entire class to explain some of the sticking points.
4. The instructor gives the groups some additional tests (measures) and instructs them to decide how they could use the tests to determine whether their test of depression is valid.
   - Students will need to apply prior knowledge of statistical methods and recognize the extent to which scores on the measures would be related to one another—depending upon whether the tests measure or do not measure depression.
5. The instructor conducts class discussion to review some of the groups' tests and methods used to determine validity and, time permitting, assigns individual writing exercise.
   - The instructor uses the end of class to help consolidate students' understanding of construct validity and the logic of validity studies.
   - Students reflect on their own understanding at the end of class— what they understood, what they didn't understand, what they found confusing.

Appendix 4.B:
How Instruction Affects Student Learning and Thinking

The following examples focus on well-known teaching techniques and how they affect student thinking (source: Barkley, Cross, & Major, 2005). For each example, I summarize the technique and identify how it engages student thinking and how the technique makes student thinking visible.

Teaching Strategy	Description of the Strategy	How the Strategy Affects Student Thinking	How/When Student Thinking Is Visible
Think-Pair-Share	The instructor poses a thought-provoking question to the class. Each student writes a response in 1–2 minutes. Students discuss their answers with a classmate sitting next to them. The interaction depends upon the instructor's goal: (1) convince the classmate that one's own answer is best, (2) create a third answer that incorporates elements of both answers, or (3) determine the strengths and limitations of each student's answer. *Optional:* The instructor asks several students to report their ideas to the entire class and uses these to make additional points or highlight key ideas. *Optional:* The instructor asks students to answer the question again in light of their discussion.	Students • try to make sense of the concepts in writing • elaborate their understanding by explaining to classmate, defending viewpoint, revising viewpoint • compare their ideas against those of other students and the instructor	• Students' written responses • Student discussions in pairs • Class discussion
Peer Instruction & ConcepTests	The instructor poses a conceptual question or problem presented in a multiple-choice format. Students take a minute or two to decide on the best answer and then use clickers to vote in class. Next each student explains/defends his or her answer to a classmate. After these paired discussions students vote again on the best answer. The instructor displays the results of the voting and explains the best choice, paying careful attention to the patterns of responses in the class.	Students • elaborate their understanding by explaining to classmate, defending and revising viewpoint • compare their ideas against those of other students and the instructor	Students compare and defend answers.
Think Aloud Pair Problem Solving (TAPPS)	TAPPS is a think aloud process in which a student says whatever comes to mind and keeps talking while answering a question or doing a task. Students participate in pairs; one acts as the problem solver, the other as listener. The problem solver reads the problem aloud and talks through his or her solution. The listener follows along and catches any errors that occur. The role of the listener is to ask for clarification but not to guide or correct the problem solver. Think alouds work best when the task or problem evokes elaborate thinking. A question or task that has a simple or single answer is not a good choice for a think aloud. The prompt does not have to be a problem in the traditional sense. For example, think alouds have been used to explore students' thinking as they read and try to make sense of historical documents.	Students • articulate their thinking about the task or problem and may discover gaps in their understanding • clarify their thinking in response to prompts from listener	Student thinking is visible throughout the think aloud activity.

Teaching Strategy	Description of the Strategy	How the Strategy Affects Student Thinking	How/When Student Thinking Is Visible
Minute Paper/ Muddiest Point Response	Students write a brief answer during or at the end of class. Usually the minute paper is used at the end of the class period (e.g, What was the most important thing you learned today?). But it could be used at any point in the class to *monitor* student thinking. For example, the instructor could ask students to explain their understanding of a key idea at a turning point in the lesson (e.g, Now that we have just discussed this topic, take a minute to write about what concept "X" means to you). *Optional*: The written answers could be used as the basis for class discussion. The instructor can ask several students to read and explain their answers.	The act of explaining is a sense-making activity. As students try to explain an idea they note connections among different facts and concepts, reorganize and restate information in their own words, and discover gaps or inconsistencies in their thinking.	Written responses reveal student thinking.
Group Discussion: Jigsaw Technique	The *jigsaw technique* is a cooperative learning strategy in which students work on a complex task or problem in groups. The problem is divided into parts, one for each member of a group. Each student serves as a specialist in one aspect of the problem and receives the resources needed to complete only his or her part of the problem. The students who are responsible for the same part of the problem join together and form a new, temporary group whose purpose is to master the concepts related to their part of the problem and develop a strategy for teaching what they have learned to the other students in their original collaborative learning group.	• Students work collectively to develop their understanding of a topic. • The act of teaching engages students in organizing information, noting connections among ideas, and explaining ideas in their own words to fellow students.	• As the groups work on the problem there are opportunities to observe the way students develop ideas and understanding of the material (e.g, when students teach their fellow group members about their part of the problem). • Unless discussion is structured so that all students participate, reticent students may be overlooked.

5

How to Study a Lesson

Data collection enables teachers to see instruction through the eyes of the students.
(Lewis, Takahashi, Murata, & King, 2003, p. 6)

This chapter explores the practices and procedures teachers can use to study class lessons. When instructors *study* the lesson, they gather evidence about how students learn, examine how the lesson supports student learning, and explore aspects of the classroom context and student behavior.

LOOKING INSIDE THE BLACK BOX: INVESTIGATING *HOW* STUDENTS LEARN AND THINK

Evaluating student performance is an integral part of teaching. We use exams, assignments, exercises, projects, and quizzes to determine students' levels of performance and to assign grades. Some instructors use formative evaluation to monitor student learning before or during instruction and use the information to modify their teaching. Ungraded quizzes, for example, can be used to help students determine what they know and don't know— *before* they take a test at the end of a unit. These are all necessary and valuable functions of evaluation, but most of the time we use assessment strategies that focus on what students learned from instruction, on the product of their learning and thinking.

Lesson study puts much less emphasis on *what* students learn, focusing instead on the learning process itself. Instructors try to gain access to student thinking to better understand how students construe the subject, where they stumble, what confuses them, how they put ideas together, how their misconceptions develop, how their thinking is affected by different parts of the lesson, and so on.

To understand lesson study as a form of inquiry, consider first how it differs from other methods used to investigate or evaluate teaching and learning (see Table 5.1). Teachers sometimes use such tools as informal

Table 5.1   Methods to Evaluate Teaching and Learning

Method of Evaluation	Primary Purposes	Description
Teacher Observation	Evaluate and/or give feedback to the instructor about teaching practices.	Fellow teacher or supervisor observes instructor during a class period. Focus is on the instructor and *teaching behaviors*.
Student Evaluation of Instruction	Evaluate the instructor and/or the course.	Students complete a questionnaire at the end of the course.
Summative Evaluation	Evaluate students to determine their achievement, assign grades, and certify proficiency.	Instructor evaluates (grades) student work or performance.
Formative Evaluation	Determine what students are learning and use it to modify instruction.	Assess student learning before, during, or after instruction and use as feedback to students and/or instructor.
Lesson Study	Examine how students learn from instruction and use it to improve instruction.	Observe students in situ during a lesson and collect additional evidence about how they interpret, interact with, and respond to the teaching, the instructor, the subject matter, and one another.

observations, impressions, and discussions with students to figure out what's going on in their classes. In contrast, lesson study involves more systematic data collection procedures as several instructors collect evidence about specific aspects of teaching and learning.

Data collection in lesson study also differs from traditional classroom observation, which tends to focus on instructor behavior. In a lesson study, the team already knows how the research lesson will be taught, so its focus is on how students respond to instruction.

Student evaluation of instruction is another common way to collect feedback about classroom teaching. Student rating forms ask students to make summary judgments at the end of the term about their perceptions of the instructor and the course.

Instructors may also use *formative assessment* consisting of assignments, exercises, quizzes, or tests as sources of evidence of how students are doing in the class. The purpose of formative assessment is to collect feedback from students and use it to adjust teaching practices. Like other forms of assessment, it tends to focus on what students learn from an instructional experience, rather than the process of learning per se (Angelo & Cross, 1993).

> **BOX 5.1**
> **Lesson Study Misconception**
>
> *Don't teachers need a thick skin to be observed and analyzed?* People who are unfamiliar with lesson study often assume that the instructor who teaches the research lesson is on the spot and subjected to unusually careful scrutiny by observers; however, lesson study is not an evaluation of the teacher's performance. As discussed in this chapter, the observation focuses on student behavior and how students react to the instruction. Moreover, the lesson is a team effort, and the other team members who co-designed the lesson tend to be excited and interested to see how the lesson turns out.

Some instructors use a pre- and postinstruction assessment at the classroom level to ascertain what students have learned. Gain scores can be used to document both student learning and teaching effectiveness.

These various methods—teacher observations, student ratings, and formative assessment—yield different types of information about teaching and learning. Observations provide a picture of teachers' behavior and instructional practices. Student evaluations indicate how students perceive instruction and their opinions about how it affects their learning. Formative assessment is used to monitor student learning and give feedback. In contrast to these methods, lesson study produces information about

1. How students respond to instruction in the context of a single lesson. Observations provide direct evidence about the interaction between teaching and learning—how teaching affects student learning and thinking.
2. How students learn the subject matter—how they interpret and construe the material, where they stumble and succeed, what confuses them, how misconceptions develop, how they put ideas together, and gaps in their thinking.

THE IMPORTANCE OF INVESTIGATING *HOW* STUDENTS LEARN

If you want to improve your teaching, what information about your students would you want to know? Would you want more summative assessment information that shows how much they learned (e.g., more test data that indicate their level of achievement for each topic)? Would you benefit from additional student evaluations of your teaching (e.g., students' perceptions of the clarity and organization of your presentations, and fairness of your grading methods)? Would it be useful to have observations of your classroom instruction by a colleague who could point out what your practices look like from the perspective of a fellow colleague? Would you want pre- and post-test scores to show you how much students learned on specific days or from entire units in a course? Would you want to know more about students' lives—who they are, their backgrounds, goals, interests? Any of these sources might give you information that could inform your practice.

These types of information often do not provide much insight into the root causes of students' difficulties. If students have difficulty following your lectures, what should you do about it? If 40% of the class fails a concept, what should you do next? We may learn something broadly about strong points and weak spots, but the types of feedback available to us in college teaching tend to be a step or two removed from where the real action is—the actual learning process. Why don't we look at the process of student learning?

We ultimately want to know more than whether or not students learned; we want to know why—the reasons that account for their learning, and in particular what accounts for their difficulties, problems, and failures. When students don't "get it," one question we need to ask is, What makes this hard? If we knew what made a concept hard, we would be better able to identify specific ways to change instruction to resolve the difficulty. To understand what makes things hard to learn, we need to look more carefully at the teaching and learning process.

Exploring a learning problem is analogous to diagnosing a medical condition. If you had a physical ailment, you would expect your physician to diagnose the problem before attempting to treat it. Moreover, the physician would be able to explain how the treatment works—by what mechanisms it brings about a cure.[1]

In education, however, there is a tendency to skip over the diagnosis and go directly to treatment. For example, you assess students at the end of a course or school year and find out they know less than you hoped they would. What's the next step? The next step is to try a different teaching

---

[1] This example is based on an ideal situation in which the causes of the physical condition are well understood, the diagnostic tests are accurate, and the treatment targets the underlying causes.

method or approach (i.e., a different treatment). But if you don't understand the underlying causes of the problem, on what basis would you decide that one treatment would be better than another? On what basis would you decide that experiential learning, for example, would work better than a didactic approach, or that a discussion would be better than a written exercise? Usually, we have little basis for making the decision. This is not to say that there isn't plenty of educational research on teaching methods. But even when research studies compare one method to another, they do not investigate the basis for any observed differences between the two. For example, in 2009 the Department of Education issued a major report that reviewed hundreds of studies comparing the outcomes of online with face-to-face classes. The report found that online classes are slightly more effective than face-to-face classes (Means, Toyama, Murphy, Bakia, & Jones, 2009). But the researchers do not know why this is the case. They speculate that the reason is greater time on task by online learners than students in face-to-face classes.

Education is similar to areas of medicine in which the underlying causes of disorders are not well understood. Consider this characterization of treatments for neuropsychiatric disorders by the 2007 Nobel Laureate in Medicine, Dr. Mario Capeechi:

> [W]ith neuropsychiatric disorders right now, we simply try drugs off the shelf. If they work, we continue to use them. If they don't work, we move on to another. But we don't have a real understanding of what that drug is doing.
>
> But once you understand how the brain works, then you will be able to design drugs that are specific. So I think you need an understanding, a deep understanding of the pathology, and then, once you have that, then you can design a drug that's very specific. (Ifill, 2007)

To borrow Capeechi's idea, in education, once we have a deeper understanding of how learning works, we will be able to design instructional strategies that are specific. Lesson study is a way teachers can explore how learning works, how their students learn in response to specific instructional practices, and how they can establish better ways to teach specific concepts in their fields. Lesson study is a way that teachers can build professional knowledge about teaching—or more specifically, *pedagogical content knowledge*, which is defined by Shulman as knowledge of

> the most useful forms of representation of [topics], the most powerful analogies, illustrations, examples, explanations, and demonstrations—in a word, the ways of representing and formulating the subject that make it comprehensible to others.

Pedagogical content knowledge also includes an understanding of what makes the learning of specific topics easy or difficult: the conceptions and preconceptions that students of different ages and backgrounds bring with them to the learning of those most frequently taught topics and lessons. (1986, p. 9; 1987, p. 9)

STUDYING A LESSON

A live lesson can be a surprisingly complex event. It usually has several parts with different purposes, activities, and materials. Students engage in the activities and material, while also interacting with the instructor and one another—and it all takes place in real time. Planning to study a lesson involves careful consideration of how to capture the interactions among the lesson's parts and the participants.

Much of the groundwork for the study takes place during lesson planning when teams identify a goal (or problem) to investigate, design a lesson to address the goal, identify what types of evidence they will gather, and create activities in the lesson to make student thinking open to observation. The next steps in preparing to study the lesson are to select and coordinate the data collection procedures. This entails deciding how to carry out the observation of the lesson and gather additional evidence.

Data collection. Observation is the primary source of evidence, and students' written work is usually used to complement or augment observations. Written work broadly includes responses to assignments—in class exercises, problem sets, group summaries, class notes, and any other pieces of student work related to the research lesson. For example, a team that plans to use a small-group exercise to promote students' analytical thinking (goal) will collect evidence of analytical thinking during the group activity (e.g., observations of how students use material from the course readings to support their ideas, or how group members challenge and support one another's ideas). The team might supplement this evidence with individual summaries written by students at the end of the activity.

Broader features of teaching and learning. A research lesson is an opportunity to observe the context in which teaching and learning take place. In addition to the specific learning goals of the lesson, teams also attend to broader features of teaching and learning. Teams can take into account how students approach the class, how they interact with one another, how they respond to the instructor, and variations in student behavior.

Many unplanned things happen during a class period. Some are relevant to student learning; others are not. Instructors should be prepared for the unexpected—unanticipated events that shed light on teaching and learning.

For example, in one of our research lessons, students worked in small groups on several tasks, and we used group summaries as evidence of understanding. Observers found that several groups were off-task during the lesson. Worse, these groups were able to fake a credible response when asked to give a group summary of their ideas. Had we not observed this activity, we might have inferred from their summaries that the group discussion was key to their understanding.

How to Observe a Lesson

Data collection techniques vary from relatively unstructured note taking to the use of checklists and rubrics. Teams adopt strategies best suited to their research lesson.

1. *Field notes.* These are detailed written notes by observers. They are a good way to record the entire lesson. When there are multiple observers, you can get detailed observations of specific students or groups of students.
2. *Focal questions.* These orient observers to key features of the lesson and student responses (e.g., "To what extent do students challenge and support one another's ideas when they work in small groups?" or "In what ways do students exhibit interest or disinterest in the lesson?"). Focal questions help ensure that observers will attend to specific aspects of the lesson. Appendix 5.A contains a list of possible focal questions.
3. *Checklists and rubrics.* Checklists are useful ways to monitor specific types of responses (e.g., the number of times students make metacognitive comments such as "I don't understand this," or "Oh, that's what he means? I was thinking just the opposite"). An advantage of a checklist or rubric is that it makes the observers' job a little easier because it describes in detail the type of activity to look for.

Appendix 5.B describes additional data collection strategies that can be used in lesson studies.

Whom to Observe

Teams may want to focus on specific individuals or groups of students (e.g., students who differ in ability and performance in the class). Or, if the lesson involves group work, the team may preselect certain groups for observation.

BOX 5.2
Video and Audio Recording

Teams sometimes record their research lessons. A video record of the lesson allows you to review lesson segments for more thorough analysis or to check on the accuracy of a specific observation. Moreover, video segments can be used to demonstrate how to teach the lesson for those interested in the topic. In some cases audio may be a better way to record the events. Recording in classrooms is often difficult. It is especially difficult to get good audio recordings throughout the room. Teams that plan to record a lesson might find it beneficial to perform a pilot test by recording in a classroom to check the quality of the video and audio you can expect to capture.

In smaller classes observers may be able to watch all of the students throughout the lesson. In larger classes where it is impossible to observe everyone, teams decide how to observe a representative sample of the class.

Coordinating the Observation

Prior to the class period, teams prepare students, observers, and the videographer for the research lesson.

1. *Prepare students.* Brief students about the research lesson prior to the day it is taught. Describe the purpose of the study and the role of the observers. Instructors who plan to present or publish their lesson study work should consult their campus Institutional Review Board (IRB) for information about informed consent. Appendix 5.C includes an example of informed consent.

2. *Prepare observers.* Teams write *observation guidelines* that observers will use during the lesson. These include a copy of the lesson plan and a detailed description of what observers should do and attend to during the lesson (e.g., take field notes, answer focal questions, and/ or use a checklist). Teams often invite outside observers (e.g., colleagues who did not participate in the lesson planning) to attend the lesson. Outside observers may not understand the purpose and focus of the study. If possible, meet with outside observers; brief them on the lesson and their role as observers.

3. *Prepare the videographer.* If you decide to record the lesson, talk to the videographer about what and how to record in the classroom. A special concern is the audio quality of the recording; video is not useful if you cannot hear the participants.

BOX 5.3
An Example of Observation Guidelines

Appendix 5.D contains a copy of the observation guidelines used by a lesson study team at UW–La Crosse. Its guidelines included the following:

1. information about the lesson—the topic, the rationale for the lesson, goals of the lesson, the lesson plan;
2. focal questions and suggestions about what to look for in the class;
3. an evaluation form with questions about how students interacted in small groups during the lesson; and
4. questions about what worked well and did not work well and suggestions for improving the lesson.

Collecting Additional Evidence

Teams often supplement their observations with students' written work, which may be done before, during, or after the lesson.

- *Work written before the lesson.* Asking students to write answers or solve problems before the lesson can provide baseline information about their initial ideas, preconceptions, and misconceptions about the topic of the lesson. These can be used as a reference point to note changes in thinking that may take place during the lesson.

- *Work written during the lesson.* Asking students to write during the lesson is a way to collect evidence from every student in the class. This exercise can add information when students do not contribute to class discussions or when observers cannot focus on every student in the class. Written responses also supplement verbal responses. A student may reveal more in a written response than in a verbal exchange in class. Conversely, a student who sounds like he has a good grasp of an idea may reveal gaps when he writes about it. Written work is also a way to collect thoughts that students do not want to make public to peers. Furthermore, a written exercise allows students a little more time to reflect and compose a response.

- *Work written after the lesson.* Asking students to write at the very end of class (e.g., a minute paper or muddiest point response) or do a homework assignment based on the lesson can provide a snapshot of how they think about the topic or what they can do with the topic (e.g., use material from the lesson to solve a problem or develop a viewpoint) directly following the lesson.

SUMMARY

Studying a lesson is a substantive investigation of teaching and learning in which teachers collect systematic evidence to better understand how the lesson supports and limits student learning. To design a study, teachers create ways to make student thinking visible, define learning goals in terms of observable behavior, and orchestrate a plan to collect data during the lesson.

The study is an opportunity for teachers to participate in a rare event: the observation of student learning in the classroom while someone else teaches the lesson. The data provide the basis for making changes to improve the lesson—and, ultimately, to improve student learning. But the study also provides the basis for teachers to learn much more about how their students learn and make sense of the subjects we teach. As one Japanese teacher said, "Lesson study is important because you develop the eyes to see students."

Is the Research Lesson Effective?

Many instructors want to know how well the lesson worked—in other words, how well students accomplished the learning goals. Table 5.2 outlines four techniques you can use to document students' achievement with respect to the lesson's learning goals.[2]

Recommendation: Understand the Lesson First; Evaluate Its Effectiveness Later

The purpose of a lesson study is to better understand how the lesson supports student learning and thinking. Unless you have a lot of lesson study experience or classroom research experience, I recommend that you postpone the

---

[2] If you intend to publish the student achievement data, I suggest you consult an assessment or educational research specialist to discuss appropriate ways to conduct the study.

Table 5.2 Strategies to Evaluate the Effectiveness of a Lesson

Goal	Technique	Benefits	Limiting Conditions
Assess students' overall level of achievement with respect to the lesson's goals.	Evaluate students at the end of the lesson.	Provides evidence about the extent to which students achieved the lesson's learning goal(s).	Does not take into account students' prior knowledge and competencies.
Assess the long-term effects of the lesson on student achievement.	Evaluate students at some later date after the lesson.	Long(er)-term assessment can provide evidence about the lasting effects of the lesson and possibly the cumulative effects of the lesson combined with other lessons and experiences.	Difficult to rule out other sources of influence on student thinking such as what students learn after the lesson.
Assess what students *gained* from the lesson.	Evaluate students before (pre) and after (post) the lesson.	Provides evidence about how much students' learning and thinking change during the lesson.	Without a comparison group, there is no basis for knowing whether the gains are better than for a different type of lesson.
Assess whether students learn as much or more from the research lesson compared with an alternative method.	Evaluate the research lesson compared with another lesson.	Provides evidence about how the lesson compares to other methods.	Requires specific conditions and procedures that are difficult to implement (e.g., Do the lessons being compared really address the same learning goals? Are the students in both groups comparable?)

BOX 5.4
Lesson Study Misconception

Lesson study is a method to test the effectiveness of teaching methods.
Japanese teachers do not do lesson studies to determine how well a
lesson works. Their focus is on understanding how teaching supports
student learning. Of course, what they learn could be used to improve
the effectiveness of the lesson. College teachers sometimes approach
lesson study with the teaching effectiveness question as a primary aim.
Some teams go so far as to compare their research lesson to a lesson
on the same topic but taught in a different format. Unfortunately, if
the teaching effectiveness question is their only concern, instructors
may miss out on the *real* lesson study experience.

---

question of effectiveness. In other words, put aside the question of *how well*
the lesson works and concentrate on *how* it works. If you gain insight into
how the lesson works, you will be in a better position to modify and improve
it. Moreover, understanding the lesson will help you develop ways to evaluate
student achievement and provide a better basis for evaluating the lesson's
effectiveness.

Appendix 5.A:
Types of Focal Questions

1. Did student thinking change during the lesson? Where did changes take place? What were the antecedents of the change?
2. What did student thinking look like during the lesson and how does it compare to what you thought it would look like?
3. What did you observe that was consistent or inconsistent with the goal(s) of the lesson?
4. When we designed the lesson we anticipated that students would have many different solutions to the problem we posed. What types of reactions did you observe and how do they compare to one another?
5. Were you surprised by students' reactions at any point in the lesson?
6. Each of you observed a different group of students. Will each of you describe and summarize the highlights of your group?
7. One of the things we wanted to see is whether students would be more actively engaged with the topic than they usually are in our classes. How would you describe the engagement of students you observed?
8. At what points in the lesson did students seem to lose interest, become confused, or disengage from the activity?
9. We hoped to see more students using the material from the reading assignment in their group discussions. To what extent did you observe this? How would you characterize their use of the material?
10. When you think about the entire lesson sequence, do you think the parts fit together as we intended them to? Were there some parts of the lesson that were unnecessary, too long, or too short?
11. We anticipated that the opening activity would elicit students' preconceptions about the topic. Do you think it did this adequately?
12. Do you think students you observed were distracted by your presence as an observer?

13. We thought that students would have particular trouble with the third question on the handout. How did the students you observed respond to it?

14. In most of our classes students give up on this task pretty easily. What did you observe this time?

15. Based on students' responses, what do you think was the most difficult part of the task?

16. We haven't had time to look at students' written responses to question 2, but how would you characterize their understanding of the topic based on their discussion of it in the small groups?

17. We decided to use structured group discussions in the lesson to support students' analysis of the topic. What were the types of thinking you observed in the groups? Were there particular strengths or weaknesses?

18. What are the similarities and differences between the responses of weaker and stronger students (or comparisons between any subsets of students)?

Appendix 5.B:
Data Collection Strategies for Student Learning, Thinking, and Behavior

These guidelines are intended for instructors who have minimal classroom observation experience. They introduce a variety of methods that teams might use to collect observational data.

Strategy	What Is Observed/Recorded	Uses/Benefits	Drawbacks
Field Notes	Detailed description of what students say and do during a class or episode	Thick, detailed description	Difficult to keep pace and record everything
Outcome-Oriented	What students say and do with respect to intended outcomes of a lesson	Focuses on outcomes of a lesson or activity; e.g., Did students draw on relevant course material?	Difficult to keep multiple questions in mind simultaneously
Focal Questions	Responses and behavior associated with specific questions	Focuses on specific aspects of a lesson or student behavior; e.g., Did students use the three examples from the reading as a basis for solving the problem in class?	May overlook other important behavior
Checklist	Frequency of listed behaviors	Records how much or how often behavior takes place in a lesson; e.g., How many times did students indicate lack of understanding?	Difficult to anticipate all important or relevant behavior Loses antecedent-consequence connections
Online Discourse	Written responses in online discussions	Instead of, or to augment observations of, face-to-face student interactions	May not be spontaneous responses
Prompted Written Responses	Students' written responses to specific prompts during class	Augments observations of students in the classroom Uses strategically in class period	Isolated snapshots of thinking at a certain moment
Think Aloud	Students as they think aloud while solving a problem or working on a task	In-depth record of how students learn and think	Time-consuming
Clinical Interview	Students' responses to a series of prompts/questions in a one-on-one interview	In-depth record of how students learn and think	Time-consuming

FIELD NOTES

Field notes are detailed descriptions of what students say and do. As an observer you act as a human recording device. This strategy is used when you want a thick, detailed description of an event. It is also used when you are uncertain about what to expect in the situation or when you do not know what might be important or unimportant—so you try to capture it all.

The benefit of field notes is that multiple observers can capture a rich record of the lesson including unanticipated events and surprises that might be overlooked with other methods. The method also preserves the chronology of events and allows you to look at antecedent-consequence relations.

A drawback is that observers can be overwhelmed by the volume of information, especially if the class is highly interactive and fast-paced. Experienced observers manage the overload problem by using their own shorthand for repetitive information, such as giving participants a number or letter rather than writing their name.

Observation vs. inference. Instructors must decide whether they want pure observation—descriptions of the class period—or whether to ask observers to include their interpretations and inferences of student activity. Trying to describe and interpret behavior simultaneously complicates the observation.

OUTCOME-ORIENTED

Observers use broad behavior categories to guide their observations. The table on page 84 identifies four types of outcomes expected in a single lesson. Instructors decide in advance which features of the lesson are most important to observe. The categories and questions direct observers' attention to these aspects of the teaching-learning episode.

A drawback to the strategy is that it can be difficult for observers to attend to multiple aspects of the lesson simultaneously. However, with practice observers can become adept at this method.

FOCAL QUESTIONS

This strategy uses more specific questions than the outcome-oriented approach. A focal question focuses on a specific behavior or activity related to the lesson (e.g., Did students use the three examples from the class reading as a basis for solving the problem given in class?).

Type of Outcome: Academic Learning and Thinking
  Characterize the strengths and weaknesses of students' thinking as reflected in
    their oral or written responses.
  Did students draw upon relevant course material?
  Where did students have difficulty, seem confused, get stuck?
  What comments or writing provide evidence they understood or
    misunderstood relevant concepts and ideas?
  What misconceptions about the subject surfaced during the lesson?

Type of Outcome: Motivation and Engagement
  Characterize students' motivation and engagement as reflected in their tone of
    voice, body language, exclamations, persistence, and comments.
  Did particular students disengage from the lesson (e.g., students who are
    especially weak or strong)?
  How did students react to complex or especially difficult parts of the material
    or activity?

Type of Outcome: Social Behavior
  Characterize the quality of peer interaction during the class.
  Did students challenge and support one another in appropriate ways?
  How did peer interaction support or interfere with students' understanding or
    performance?

Type of Outcome: Student Attitudes Toward Learning
  Characterize the participation of several students who differ with respect to
    interest and level of achievement in the subject.
  Did students appear interested in or excited about the lesson?
  Do students want to learn more about the topic?

Adapted from Lewis, C. (2002b). *Lesson Study: A Handbook of Teacher-Led Instructional Change*, Philadelphia, PA:
Research for Better Schools.

Use focal questions when you want to know about very specific aspects of student thinking and behavior, especially when you anticipate that the lesson will induce a change in student thinking. A drawback is that you may overlook important events that are not covered by your questions.

CHECKLIST

A checklist itemizes behaviors of interest. Observers note the frequency of the behavior (e.g., the number of times students indicate that they don't understand or are confused), usually by ticking off instances of the behaviors on the checklist. Alternatively, a checklist might require the observer to categorize behavior. For example, instructors might want to know the number *and* types of *meta-understanding* statements students make during the class. A *meta-understanding* statement is a comment in which students reveal awareness of or attempts to regulate their own understanding. Some examples include, "I think I understand this now," "This is too complicated; I don't get it," and "I need to reread the material because I don't follow this at all." Observers may note the frequency of certain types of behavior *and* record the type—write them down.

Checklists are easy to use and useful when instructors want to know the frequency and variety of certain behaviors. There are two disadvantages of the checklist strategy. First, it can be difficult to anticipate the most important things that will take place during a class period. Your checklist can miss pivotal events during the lesson. Second, the checklist method loses the connection between the behavior and its antecedent. You may learn that students claimed to be confused 50 times during the class but you won't know the source of their confusion.

Below is a type of checklist I have used to evaluate class discussions. It specifies some types of productive and counterproductive behavior that typify group discussions.

The checklist could be used to note the frequency of each behavior for the entire group or to keep track of one or more members of the group.

WRITTEN DISCOURSE

Digital tools can be used to *observe* student thinking outside the classroom. The written responses of students participating in an online discussion can be used as evidence of their thinking at various points in learning a topic.

Checklist: Incidence of Productive and Counterproductive Discussion Behavior

___ asked, gave information
___ asked, gave reactions
___ asked, answered questions
___ restated ideas/points in articles
___ restated ideas/points of discussants
___ asked for/gave examples
___ asked for/gave summary
___ asked for/gave evidence or support for ideas
___ redirected group to return to task
___ monitored time
___ encouraged, supported other ideas
___ elaborated on others' ideas

___ monopolized discussion
___ called attention to self
___ chronically made interruptions
___ criticized others (put down)
___ changed subject often
___ frequently made irrelevant comments
___ was withdrawn, did not participate
___ was apologetic
___ OTHER—please specify:

An advantage of the online strategy is that instructors can trace the development of concepts in one or more students in a sequence of online postings. A potential disadvantage of this method is that students' responses may not be spontaneous.

THINK ALOUDS

A *think aloud* is a procedure used in the cognitive sciences to study learning and thinking during problem solving. The student is trained to think aloud while she or he solves a problem or completes a task. College instructors can adapt it to investigate student thinking. Training students is relatively easy—give them the task and tell them to say out loud everything that comes to mind as they work through it. Initially students may be self-conscious or tend to stop talking. Usually a monitor is present to urge students to keep talking whenever they hit a dead zone. With practice students become less self-conscious and more adept at thinking aloud.

The think aloud is a powerful tool to explore student thinking in depth. The major drawback is that it is time-consuming, but there are several ways to reduce the time involved:

1. Use student assistants to record and monitor the problem solver. Students could do this during tutoring sessions.
2. Use think aloud paired problem solving in class. Set up think alouds in class where students take turns in pairs being the problem solver and monitor. Observers can focus on student pairs.
3. Have students record themselves doing think alouds. If students are well versed in thinking aloud you might entrust them to record themselves. We are currently experimenting with the use of Jing, a free, screencast software that allows you to record the contents on your computer monitor and include audio narration. Students can make short videos (up to 5 minutes) of themselves thinking through a task, question, or problem.

There is no reason to do think alouds with large numbers of students. You can uncover typical patterns of thinking, misconceptions, and preconceptions using a handful of students. However, consider selecting students whom you think might produce very different responses (e.g., students who differ in ability—strong vs. weak students in a class; majors vs. non-majors).

CLINICAL INTERVIEW

A clinical interview is a structured interaction in which an interviewer presents a task or specific questions to a student. The student answers each question and the interviewer follows up with additional questions intended to probe student thinking. It is a powerful way to explore student thinking, but it is time intensive. The interview is not a viable lesson study strategy unless the lesson itself is organized in an interview-type format, such as Socratic questioning.

Appendix 5.C:
Example of Informed Consent

If you plan to present or publish your lesson study work consult your campus Institutional Review Board (IRB). Your IRB may require a proposal to conduct a study with human subjects. Unless approved in advance by the IRB you may not be able to use data from your lesson study for research purposes. *Informed consent* is a procedure in which you inform students about your study and ask their permission to use their work and performance as data. The consent form presented here is one approved at UW–La Crosse. You should consult your campus IRB for local requirements.

Informed Consent for Students in the UW–La Crosse Lesson Study Project
Permission to Use Course Work for Research Purposes

This semester I am working with several other instructors to study how students learn [*Insert your information*]. On one or more class days, we will videotape the class period and collect additional information about your learning. Several instructors may be present to observe the class and they may ask you questions about your experiences that day. Our goal is to better understand how students learn from our teaching and then use that information to improve instruction in the course.

It is likely that some aspects of this project will be presented or published in the future. In keeping with the ethical standards for doing research with human subjects, I am requesting your written permission to include excerpts, examples and portions of your course work—both written and videotaped—for future presentations and publication purposes. Your identity will remain confidential and none of the written material will be identified with you individually. You also have the option not to be in the final edited version of any video clips we produce for this project.

It is perfectly acceptable not to grant permission to use your work for these purposes, and I assure you that your decision will not adversely affect my opinion of you or your experience in the class.

I have been informed that:

- the purpose of this study is to investigate how college students learn [*Insert your material*] and to improve teaching in the course.
- one or more class periods may be videotaped and outside observers may be present in the class to gather information and interview students.
- examples of my written work and videotaped segments of me in the class may be used in publications and presentations, and that none of the material will be identified with me individually.
- I can chose not to be in the final, edited version of video clips produced in this study.
- There will be no penalty if I decide not to give permission to use my course material for the study.

If you have any questions about the study procedures please contact me at [*Insert your information*]. Questions regarding the protection of human subjects may be addressed to [*Insert your information*], Chair of the Institutional Review Board for the Protection of Human Subjects, [*Insert contact information*].

Please sign and return this form at the beginning of class, [*Insert date*]

I GIVE my permission to use portions of my course work including videotape clips of me in class for publication and presentation purposes.

Student Participant_____ Date_____
Instructor/Investigator_____ Date_____

I DO NOT give my permission to use portions of my course work for publication and presentation purposes.

Student Participant_____ Date_____
Instructor/Investigator_____ Date_____

Appendix 5.D:
Example of Observation Guidelines for a Research Lesson in Psychology

In addition to this protocol observers receive a copy of the research lesson plan.

OBSERVATION PROTOCOL: CONSTRUCT VALIDITY RESEARCH LESSON

The purpose of having several instructors observe the class is to gather as much information about the process of the lesson as possible. Your primary task is to observe **how the students respond to the lesson and make some conclusions about how the LESSON worked.** In other words, the primary focus of your observation is student thinking and student behavior. Of less importance is what the instructor does because we have already planned the lesson in some detail and know what the instructor is supposed to do.

You will be observing one group of approximately four students. Please *do not* make comments to or help your group. If students try to interact with you just remind them that you are an observer and not a participant in the lesson (e.g., do not answer questions or clarify instructions).

Specific focus of observation. The major learning goal of the lesson is for students to understand the *logic* underlying validation studies of construct validity. Pay careful attention to (and record) the way students describe and explain the basis for their predictions of how subjects in the studies will perform. We would like to get a good record of how they construe and make sense of the concepts regardless of whether their reasoning is well developed, incomplete, or tangled. Note any changes in their thinking, moments of insight or recognition, misconceptions, and difficulties they have.

General focus of observation. Many things take place during a lesson that can influence student learning and thinking. Please take detailed field notes of your group and whole-class discussion. Note such things as

- student interest and engagement in the lesson (e.g., staying on task, persisting during difficulty, evidence of boredom, evidence of enjoyment, evidence of responding to a challenge);
- quality of interpersonal interaction (e.g., dominating members, quiet members, level of participation, distractions);
- quality of group discussion and discourse (e.g., how group members exchange and respond to ideas; probe for better understanding; accept statements at face value; ask questions to clarify; ignore statements; make meta-comments such as, "I still don't get this," or "Something is missing; that doesn't seem right"); and
- other aspects of the lesson that influence the quality of the experience.

CONSTRUCT VALIDITY

Observer Reactions to the Lesson

Now that you have observed the lesson, please rate the following statements, and answer questions 8 and 9.

	Totally Disagree						Totally Agree
1. All members participated in the process.	1	2	3	4	5	6	7
2. The group was able to stay on track with the lesson (i.e., did not derail, discussing irrelevant information).	1	2	3	4	5	6	7
3. The group seemed confused about the technical processes of the lesson.	1	2	3	4	5	6	7
4. The group seemed confused about the concepts the lesson was addressing.	1	2	3	4	5	6	7
5. The group seemed to understand the *concept* of construct validity.	1	2	3	4	5	6	7
6. The group seemed to understand the concept of "construct".	1	2	3	4	5	6	7
7. The group seemed to understand the *logic* of construct validity.	1	2	3	4	5	6	7

8. Given your observations, what aspects of the lesson need to be changed? How could the lesson be improved?

9. What aspects of the lesson should remain the same? What worked well?

6

Analyzing and Revising the Lesson

Think of a lesson study as an exploratory study during which you try to learn as much as you can about how students respond to the lesson. The purpose of analyzing the lesson is to learn as much as possible from the evidence and use it to inform practice. The analysis addresses three broad concerns:

1. How did students respond to the lesson? In what ways did students accomplish the learning goals of the lesson or overcome the learning problem? In what ways did the lesson support student learning, thinking, and engagement?
2. What does the evidence suggest about how to improve the lesson?
3. What did the team members learn about teaching and student learning from the experience?

Analysis of the lesson takes place in two parts. First, hold a debriefing meeting during which participants discuss their observations and comment on the lesson. Second, further analyze observational evidence and examine additional data such as students' written responses to questions or exercises.

ANALYSIS PART 1: THE DEBRIEFING MEETING

Team members and observers hold a meeting to discuss the lesson after it is taught. This meeting should take place while the experience is still fresh in the observers' minds, preferably within a day or two of the lesson. The debriefing session's purpose is for participants to share and interpret their observations, and to examine the implications for improving the lesson. The debriefing is also a wide-ranging discussion about any aspects of the lesson of interest to the participants.

To take full advantage of the debriefing opportunity, team members should prepare material and establish some ground rules to guide the debriefing session. These may include the following:

- Prepare a handout for participants with key questions and topics team members want to discuss during the debriefing.
- Remind participants to bring important material to the session including their observation notes.
- Designate a meeting facilitator to keep the group on task and move the discussion forward. Teams can get sidetracked on one or two issues and neglect other important aspects of the lesson.
- Designate someone to take careful notes during the session and to collect the additional data from lesson observers.
- Decide on any preferred format or protocol for the discussion. Some groups may want to address questions or hear from participants in a certain order.

BOX 6.1

Japanese teachers often hold their debriefing session immediately after the lesson is taught. They refer to it as a *colloquium* during which the lesson study teacher, group members, and outside observers discuss the research lesson. The person who taught the lesson is given the opportunity to speak first, followed by lesson study group members and other observers. The discussion focuses on the lesson (not the teacher) and on analyzing what, how, and why students learned or did not learn from the experience.

The debriefing session should be an in-depth discussion about how the lesson worked, that is, how it supported student learning, thinking, and engagement. The aim of the analysis is also to develop evidence-based revisions to improve the lesson. Teams need to balance these two aspects of analysis. Sometimes teachers are eager to offer suggestions about how to "fix" the lesson. It is important to focus on understanding the lesson before revising it. Of course, some fixes are minor and don't change the overall lesson significantly. For example, someone might notice that the instructions on a handout are confusing and recommend changes to improve them. In these cases, the team can note the change and then resume with other issues. However, sometimes instructors propose changes that would fundamentally change the lesson. Team members should try to postpone talking about major revisions until they have a thorough understanding of the lesson.

The debriefing meeting is a unique experience for college teachers. Teachers may be accustomed to observing colleagues' classes and being observed by others, but most have never experienced a working session in which multiple observers collectively recount their observations, interpret students' actions, and try to explain how learning takes place. For many teachers in the College Lesson Study Project (CLSP) observing the lesson and participating in the debriefing session are highlights of their experience. It is a long awaited opportunity to examine how their lesson design turns out. Outside observers also report that the observation and debriefing are interesting and unique experiences.

ANALYSIS PART 2: DRILLING DOWN

After the debriefing session teams decide whether they need or want to do any further analysis of evidence. Usually teams meet again to discuss their observations further and consider additional evidence they collected from the lesson.

Lesson studies produce extensive observations of the entire lesson as well as observations that focus on focal questions (e.g., what parts of the concept were most difficult for students) and specific students or groups of students (e.g., strong, weak, nonnative English speakers, majors, nonmajors). Additionally, teams may collect written student responses to prompts or exercises and results of checklists or observers' rating forms.

To systematize their data, teams may

1. develop rubrics to organize and analyze qualitative differences among students' responses and actions;
2. focus on observations of pivotal moments in the lesson when changes in student thinking did or did not take place as anticipated;
3. examine the entire sequence of lesson activities to determine how they contributed to student learning; and
4. examine extremes in student performance by comparing responses of students who struggled with the topic with responses of those who appeared to have little difficulty.

Subsequent analysis can involve establishing guidelines or rubrics to evaluate students' written work, compiling results from checklists or observation protocols, and holding one or more team meetings to collectively discuss team findings.

ANALYZING OBSERVATIONAL DATA

Analysis of observations will vary depending upon whether the team used a structured or unstructured approach. In a structured approach, all observers might focus on the same aspects of the lesson and student behavior. For example, each observer might watch a small group of students complete a task during the lesson and focus on how the students use course material to come up with solutions. The team then compiles and compares observations to determine how most students responded to the task. In unstructured observations, observers record as much activity as they can. Subsequent analysis might consist of observers taking turns describing their findings and highlighting significant activity. Observations produce a wealth of detailed information. During the meeting, group members try to decide which aspects of the observations are most interesting and relevant to the lesson's goals.

In both structured and unstructured observations, instructors look for patterns in students' behavior and responses to instruction. For example, the team may be especially interested in how students explain a key concept during the lesson. The team's analysis would focus on what characteristics the student explanations have in common as well as patterns of differences in explanations.

ANALYZING STUDENTS' WRITTEN WORK

Students' written work can broaden and deepen the picture of student thinking. It can corroborate or help to interpret in-class observations and gain access to information that is not made visible in class. Samples can include responses to questions, homework problems, quizzes, class notes, in-class exercises, postlesson reflections or homework, and group summaries.

Typically, written work analysis involves establishing guidelines or rubrics to help classify and identify patterns of responses. This process may resemble what instructors do when they evaluate and grade students' work. In a lesson study, instructors put grading aside and focus on those aspects of students' work most relevant to the lesson's goals. For example, a group of psychology instructors wanted to characterize the quality of students' written explanations during a lesson. They decided that three levels or types of explanations were sufficient for their purposes (see Table 6.1).

The most underdeveloped responses were not explanations, but material and topic descriptions. Distinct from these responses were responses in which students started to see how the course material could be used to

Table 6.1 Example of Rubric for Student Explanations Produced During a Research Lesson

Type of Explanation	Characteristics
Well-Developed	Response incorporates course material Connections among ideas are relevant and appropriate.
Emerging	Responses incorporates course material Connections among ideas may be flawed, tangled, or incomplete.
Not an Explanation	Student describes or talks around the topic but does not form an explanation. Response exhibits person-on-the-street quality—does not include course material in response

explain a concept. Such responses were still under development and contained flaws, gaps, and some misunderstandings. A third type of explanation revealed a reasonable understanding of the topic. Students made relevant and appropriate connections. Still, these were not necessarily high-level, precise, or flawless explanations. The rubric represents a way to characterize students' thinking along a continuum ranging from seriously underdeveloped to a well-developed grasp of the topic and gives the team a rough and ready measure of the variability in students' responses.

USING EVIDENCE TO REFINE THE LESSON

Lesson study involves evidence-based improvement of teaching and learning. Most lesson studies involve two iterations of the research lesson so teams have two opportunities to analyze and reflect on ways to revise the lesson. These ideas are incorporated into the second iteration of the lesson. The revisions can range from minor refinements to a major overhaul of the lesson. Most teams make several substantive changes in their design and materials. In the CLSP, there have been teams that have put aside their first lesson plan and started over from scratch. After teams teach and analyze the revised lesson (second iteration) they identify final revisions and document them in a lesson study report.

By charting the process by which students learn, instructors can pinpoint where and why students have difficulties, what aspects of the subject matter cause problems, and how instructional activities support or do not support their progress. This can provide specific evidence that instructors can use to refine their teaching methods.

EXAMPLES OF USING EVIDENCE TO MAKE REVISIONS

The following examples describe how instructors used observational evidence as a basis for revising their research lesson.

Example 1

Introductory psychology students tend to explain human behavior in terms of one dominant factor or reason and disregard other possible sources of influence (e.g., "depression is caused by low self-esteem"). Psychology instructors designed a lesson to promote the use of multiple factors to explain social behavior and collected examples of students' explanations of social behavior before, during, and after the research lesson took place.

Pre- and postlesson comparisons showed a marked improvement in students' use of multiple factors to explain social behavior. Based on this evidence, the lesson appeared to have worked well; however, observations during the lesson revealed that students had reservations about whether the factors they cited were of any real importance. In the words of one student, "There are all these factors and everything, but I think what really matters is what kind of person you are. If you are a caring person you will help people; if not you don't." This sentiment directly contradicted the point of the lesson, which was to demonstrate that social context plays a powerful role in human actions. This student was able to explain behavior in terms of social influences but clung to the "Good Person Theory" as the *real* explanation. Based on these findings, the instructors developed additional scenarios for the research lesson intended to create dissonance in student thinking (e.g., examples in which *good* people actually do bad things and *bad* people do good things). They also decided to embed more scenarios throughout the unit in the course to expose students to many cases that illustrate how social context affects human actions.

Example 2

Instructors designed a lesson in which students listened to a short lecture and then worked in small groups for most of the class period. In the final 15 minutes, each group gave a brief, oral summary to the entire class. One observer reported that a group he watched during the class period did not do the assigned task at all. Instead, several students worked on homework for a different class and two other students talked to each other about something unrelated to the task at hand. Five minutes before the oral summaries started, one student in the group volunteered to give the group's presentation. The student gave a credible performance, and the instructor was completely unaware that the group had not done the assignment.

In the debriefing meeting, the team had a lengthy discussion about the task and came to the realization that it was not sufficiently challenging to sustain a full class period. Furthermore, there was no individual accountability in the groups, which made it easy for students not to participate. They also recognized that the oral summary process was ineffective. By the time two to three groups delivered their summaries, there was very little new for the remaining groups to say or add. The instructors revised the assignment to include more challenging questions. They redesigned the end of the class period. They dropped the oral group summaries, and instead asked each student to write an individual summary. The instructor then led a class discussion asking students to answer questions based on their written answers.

These examples illustrate the importance of observing the learning process and the value of using multiple sources of evidence. In Example 1, observations of students revealed that they could do the class assignment but did not fully accept the concepts on which it was based, and that some preferred their own theories. In Example 2, observations revealed that students could bluff their way through the assignment without doing it at all. The observations and additional evidence provided enough detail about the learning process so that instructors could identify likely weaknesses and propose alternative strategies to support better learning.

A NOTE ABOUT LESSON STUDY AND EDUCATIONAL RESEARCH

It is important to reiterate that lesson study is practitioner inquiry and does not necessarily incorporate all the tools of formal educational research (e.g., concerns with sampling, establishing the validity of instruments, and using inferential statistics). Nor does it try—as formal educational research does—to establish results that apply to all contexts and conditions. Instead, lesson study entails naturalistic observations of students in a complex learning environment. This does not diminish its value as a tool for producing knowledge about teaching and learning. In fact, as I have suggested, lesson study is especially well suited for investigating how students learn, which is key to evidence-based improvement of teaching and learning.

In the CLSP, some teams have approached lesson study interested solely in talking about teaching and learning. Lesson study provides a well-structured approach for teaching improvement conversations. Some teams

---

BOX 6.2
Lesson Study Misconception

Lesson study is a weak form of educational research. One criticism of lesson study is that it is not a rigorous method of educational research. However, this criticism misconstrues the nature and purposes of lesson study. Teams decide individually what they want to get out of the lesson study experience. Some simply want to have sustained and substantive conversations about teaching and learning; others are equally concerned about building new knowledge about teaching. As a form of practitioner inquiry, lesson study can be molded to the interests and goals of participants. Some lesson studies are sufficiently rigorous to be published in peer-reviewed journals and presented at professional conferences. (See Becker, Ghenciu, Horak, & Schroeder, 2008; Chick, Hassel, & Haynie, 2009; Lewis, Perry, & Murata, 2006; Roback, Chance, Legler, & Moore, 2006.)

---

emphasize the systematic nature of their inquiry and look ahead to sharing their work in presentations and publications. Teams can build greater or more formal methodological rigor into their lesson studies if they choose. Some attend to the validity and reliability of their data collection strategies. For example, teams can increase the reliability of their data collection strategies or their rubrics by holding norming sessions in which instructors use guidelines or rubrics to evaluate student learning and then examine their results to look for consistencies and inconsistencies in applying the criteria and standards. Others use some pre- and postlesson data collection to document learning gains.

Perhaps the best test of a lesson study's quality is whether it satisfies the instructors' goals and whether instructors view it as a rewarding and productive experience. In my view, lesson studies are valuable to the extent that they

1. help instructors better understand how students learn in the context of the lesson's goals or problem;
2. provide evidence that can be used to improve the lesson; and
3. help participants to learn things that can be applied more widely to their teaching practice.

7

Documenting and Sharing Lesson Studies

As teams near completion of their lesson study, they look ahead to documenting and disseminating their work and ask themselves questions such as, "Have we learned something that would be of interest to others?" "How can I include the work I have done in my annual review?" "Should we develop a conference presentation?" "Is this work publishable?" "How can I pull together our materials so I can use them again in the future?" This chapter describes different ways to document lesson studies and offers examples and models for representing the work depending upon your purposes and the audiences that will receive it. There are at least three main reasons to document your lesson study work:

1. to consolidate and preserve your work for future use;
2. to demonstrate teaching improvement activities as needed for personnel decisions; and
3. to make your work accessible so other teachers can critique, use, and build upon it.

PRESERVING WORK FOR FUTURE USE

If for no other reason, teachers should document their lesson studies to consolidate what they learn from the experience and to preserve the work for future use. During a lesson study, teams usually create several types of artifacts including a detailed lesson plan, handouts and other lesson materials, a summary of their research findings, and research tools. These items comprise a rich representation of the lesson and how it worked.

By describing their research lesson in detail, teams make it readily available for use in subsequent courses. Teams can also append their notes about how to teach the lesson and include any final suggested revisions they would make. Moreover, the lesson materials may be relevant to other lessons and courses. For example, an observation protocol or checklist can be used in other courses.

> **BOX 7.1**
> **Document Your Work Throughout the Lesson Study**
>
> To make the culmination of your work considerably easier, try to document your work during the final iteration of the lesson study. Assign responsibility to group members to prepare final, revised versions of the research lesson plan and lesson materials. Draft a final version of the lesson analysis and include final conclusions and recommendations about the lesson. Teams that fail to draft the final lesson and analysis while the ideas are still fresh find it difficult to return to the work at a later date.

DEMONSTRATING TEACHING IMPROVEMENT

Most college teachers need to provide evidence of teaching effectiveness and improvement for their annual reviews and decisions that are related to their retention, tenure, and promotion. A well-written explanation of a lesson study can be a compelling artifact for this purpose. The final section in this chapter—"The Final Lesson Study Report—describes how teachers can document a lesson study to demonstrate teaching effectiveness and improvement.

MAKING WORK ACCESSIBLE: SCHOLARSHIP OF TEACHING AND LEARNING (SoTL)

A third reason to document your lesson study is to make it accessible to other teachers, who can learn from it and build upon it. Teachers who teach the same courses and topics would likely be interested in your findings even if their teaching contexts differ from yours. A lesson study that sheds light on subjects that are challenging for students to learn and difficult to teach will be of interest to fellow teachers. A lesson study can be documented as a scholarly product that can help advance teaching in one's field. Teams at University of Wisconsin campuses produce professional presentations and publications based on the lesson study work (see Becker, Ghenciu, Horak, & Schroeder, 2008; Chick, Hassel, & Haynie, 2009).

Teams produce a great deal of material as they progress through their lesson study, and these products can be used for multiple purposes. This idea of shaping the work to different purposes appeals to many instructors who are concerned not only about their own classroom teaching, but about being able to represent their work as evidence of teaching improvement and present their work as scholarly activity.

Documenting Lesson Study Material for Future Use

The team's final products can be organized into a collection of materials including the final lesson plan and class handouts. The lesson plan is particularly useful if it is a detailed account of the lesson with references and annotations about what materials to use, how to use them, and what to expect from students. When it comes time to teach the topic again in a subsequent class, team members will have a detailed record of what to do, how to do it, and what to anticipate from the class. This will result in a lesson that you can pull off the shelf when you need it. Another benefit of thoroughly documenting the lesson is that instructors around the world can use it. In the College Lesson Study Project (CLSP) we created an online gallery to archive lesson study materials (http://www.uwlax.edu/sotl/lsp/gallery.htm). Some teams have received requests from instructors at other institutions asking permission to use the lesson in their classes. A well-documented lesson can be adopted and adapted readily by instructors to fit their specific circumstances.

Documenting a Lesson Study for One's Retention, Tenure, and Promotion Portfolio

As mentioned, lesson study is substantive professional work that should be considered when making retention, promotion, and tenure decisions. In traditional research and scholarship there are clearly defined genres and conventions for documenting work for peer review. Not so in teaching. Consequently, campus review committees ask instructors to include all kinds of teaching artifacts in their files (e.g., course syllabi, assignments, exams, grade distributions, student evaluations, a teaching philosophy). Unfortunately, a loose collection of artifacts is difficult for reviewers to interpret, analyze, and evaluate. Unless instructors provide a conceptual framework and annotation for their work, reviewers may not fully grasp the individual artifacts or their cumulative significance.

One solution to this problem is to tell a brief, coherent story about your teaching based on a lesson study. The CLSP does this by using a format called the Teaching Improvement Profile (TIP) (Cerbin, 2005b). Though lesson study is a collaborative activity, the TIP allows each team member to tell about his or her individual experience. The profile takes into account three important conditions:

1. *Coherence.* A well-developed profile is a coherent story about teaching and learning. It is like a research report or case study that connects all the teaching elements—vision and goals for student learning, instructional design, teaching practices and class interactions, learning outcomes, and analysis and revision of practices.
2. *Complexity.* A well-developed profile depicts the substance and complexity of teaching *and* learning, including the goals for student learning, the rationale for one's instructional decisions, ways to observe changes in student thinking, how to evaluate the depth of their learning, and how to revise teaching to further support student learning.
3. *Brevity.* The profile is brief so that others can read it quickly. In most cases you can write a well-developed profile in three to four pages.

The TIP template is a detailed framework to report your work and includes prompts to help you include specific kinds of material in the profile (see Appendix 7.B). The profile is intended to be a comprehensive framework but instructors can modify it and adapt material to their specific institutional requirements and circumstances. Appendix 7.C contains an example of a TIP that I wrote based on my lesson study experience.

Documenting a Lesson Study as Scholarly Work

In Japan, lesson study is an important vehicle for building a professional knowledge base for teaching (see Box 7.2). Teachers share their work widely, providing a rich foundation for learning to teach. Writing about education in the United States, Hiebert, Gallimore, and Stigler (2002) note, "As much as they might benefit from the knowledge of their colleagues, most teachers have not accessed what others know and must start over, creating this knowledge anew." In higher education there has been a vibrant movement to build SoTL over the past 15 years, resulting in widespread classroom inquiry across the disciplines. However, we are a long way from anything like a professional knowledge base for teaching in our various subject areas. Lesson study could be a way to support such a knowledge base.

Imagine a set of field-tested lessons for the core concepts and topics in a course you teach. And, imagine that each lesson came with detailed information about how to teach the lesson, how students typically perform, and

---

BOX 7.2

The Japanese Model: Reports That Advance the Practice of Teaching

A Japanese lesson study report is a richly detailed description of the lesson and analysis of how the lesson worked. In it, teachers suggest ways to teach the lesson, offer insights about student learning and thinking, and discuss what they learned from the lesson study. Sometimes schools produce research bulletins that "assemble all the study lessons taught at the school during the course of the year and summarize the ideas and insights that working on the lessons provided the teachers" (Fernandez & Yoshida, 2004, p. 15).

Lesson study reports are disseminated throughout the country. They are used at local education centers where teachers receive inservice training, and many reports are published and sold in national bookstores. Each year the Japanese National Institute for Educational Research compiles more than 4,000 research papers written by teachers. Together these writings provide an extensive repository of professional knowledge and ideas from which teachers engaged in lesson study can learn and build. Clearly, through this well-developed system of publications, teachers from all corners of Japan can learn from each other's lesson study activities (Fernandez & Yoshida, 2004).

---

suggestions for improving the lesson. Rather than create lessons from scratch, instructors could adapt these lessons to their own circumstances and refine them for future use and for use by others. Of course, we do not have field-tested lessons in "ready-to-use" form. There are many curricular and teaching materials available to instructors. For example, ancillary materials for textbooks provide tips, suggestions, examples of assignments, and multimedia materials. In many disciplines, there are journals that publish work about teaching. However, there are no fully developed lessons built around the learning goals and problems related to specific topics in specific courses.

Rather than a loose collection of curricular materials, a lesson study depicts the interaction between instructional practices and student learning of specific content in specific contexts. Lesson study is a method through which teachers can build the kind of *pedagogical content knowledge* that could not only improve their own teaching but move the practice of teaching forward in their fields.

THE FINAL LESSON STUDY REPORT: A GENRE FOR THE SCHOLARSHIP OF TEACHING AND LEARNING

In the CLSP, we promote lesson study as one way to build and share professional knowledge about college teaching. The Final Lesson Study Report is a format or genre for documenting lesson studies and making the work public in a form that other teachers can critique, use, and build upon. If they so choose, teams can submit their reports to the project's online gallery to make them accessible to others.

Clearly, lesson study is not only a way to improve the teaching of those who participate in the process, but also a way to improve the practice of teaching more generally. Teachers can draw upon others' work for ideas about how to teach and how to better understand student learning.

The Final Report Format

The report format is based on two assumptions. First, it assumes that lesson study is scholarly inquiry. As such, the report must include more than a description of the research lesson—it must also be an account of the study that explains the authors' method used to study the lesson, along with their analysis, findings, and conclusions. Second, the report format assumes that the report stands on its own as a scholarly product. The report format does not fit neatly into any existing genres of research articles; nonetheless, the report captures the substance and complexity of the inquiry, and should be evaluated on its own merits as scholarly work.

The report includes three major parts: (a) Background information about the lesson; (b) the lesson plan, handouts, and related materials; and (c) the study, which analyzes how the lesson worked. Appendix 7.A contains the Final Lesson Study Report Template.

Part 1: Background

This section includes identifying information about the lesson study such as title, authors, the discipline, course description, and a 250- to 400-word executive summary.

Part 2: The Lesson

This section includes a detailed lesson plan that describes the instructional activities, what the instructors and students will do throughout the lesson, and how to teach the lesson. Instructors also describe the learning goals and discuss how the lesson is supposed to work, that is, a theoretical rationale of how the instructional activities are designed to support student learning.

Part 3: The Study

This section describes the data collection procedures and the types of evidence collected. In the Findings and Discussion sub-sections, the authors summarize and analyze the evidence, then discuss what the evidence reveals about student learning (e.g., how student thinking changed during the lesson; what types of difficulties students experience; turning points in student thinking). Based on the evidence, instructors identify further revisions to the lesson and any remaining questions or concerns.

References and Appendices

The report also includes a reference section and appendices that contain materials such as handouts, exercises, and observation protocols.

Disseminating and Sharing Lesson Study Work

It is relatively easy to make lesson studies accessible online. The CLSP online gallery, for example, hosts a collection of lesson studies by instructors from the University of Wisconsin System campuses. Lesson study teams can use their own campus sites to host their lesson study work. An alternative is to add your lesson study to the collections of learning materials hosted by Multimedia Educational Resource for Learning and Online Teaching (MER LOT.org). An added advantage of MERLOT is that materials may be peer reviewed if they meet certain criteria.

Presentations at professional conferences and publication of lesson study work in teaching-related disciplinary journals are also becoming more common (see the reference section at the end of this volume for examples).

One of the most valuable ways to share your work is to involve your colleagues by inviting them to observe a research lesson and participate in the postlesson debriefing discussion. Additionally, teams often give a departmental or campuswide colloquium. Because lesson study encompasses so many aspects of teaching and learning, it can open up conversations about learning goals, alternative teaching practices, instructors' beliefs about student learning, teaching problems instructors encounter, how to assess and evaluate student learning, and how to use assessment results to improve teaching and student performance.

Appendix 7.A:
Final Lesson Study Report Template

PART I: BACKGROUND

Title: Write a descriptive title for your lesson study so that others may cite your work (e.g., "Reading for Complexity: Recognizing and Valuing Ambiguity in Literature").

Authors: Include the names and institutional affiliations of each person on your lesson study team.

Contact: Include the name and e-mail address of a person who may be contacted about your lesson study.

Discipline or Field: If your lesson may be used in more than one discipline or field, list all that apply.

Date: Include the date you posted (or last updated) your final lesson study.

Course Name: Give the course title rather than its catalog number (e.g., Freshman Composition rather than English 110).

Course Description: Briefly describe the course, its place in the curriculum, and where the lesson fits in the course. Include pertinent facts such as course level, class size, student population, lesson length, and learning environment (e.g., networked classroom, lecture hall, special equipment).

Executive Summary: In approximately 250–450 words, provide an overview of your learning goals, instructional design, and major findings about student learning.

PART II: THE LESSON: HOW TO TEACH THE LESSON

Describe the steps of the lesson, providing enough detail so that other teachers can re-create it in their classes. Include any necessary pre- or post-lesson work. For each step in the lesson, describe instructional and learning activities that take place, including the approximate time needed for each segment of the lesson.

- Describe what teachers should do. Provide specific wording of prompts, explanations of handouts, etc.
- Describe what students should do, and how they are likely to respond. Offer tips for responding to student questions, confusions, etc.

Student Learning Goals

- List your student learning goals. Include both the immediate academic learning goals and the long-term qualities the lesson supports (e.g., abilities, skills, dispositions, sensibilities, values you want students to develop in your program). Write the goals in terms of the knowledge and qualities students should exhibit as a result of the lesson.
- Provide background on why you chose the lesson topic and your student learning goals.

How the Lesson Is Intended to Work

Discuss how the lesson is supposed to work in practice:

- Explain how the instructional and learning activities and materials are designed to facilitate and support student thinking. If applicable, discuss how you tailored the lesson for the student population, learning environment, etc.
- Refer to any theoretical, empirical, or pedagogical work that influenced your lesson design.

PART III: THE STUDY

Approach

- Describe the types of evidence you collected before, during, and after the lesson, for example observations, written work, and student interviews.
- Describe the procedure for observing the lesson, indicate who observed, what they observed, how they recorded observations, etc.

Findings

- Summarize the evidence. Present major patterns and tendencies, key observations, or representative examples of student learning and thinking.

Discussion

Discuss what your study suggests about

- how the lesson affected or changed student thinking, especially with respect to the lesson's goals;
- what the lesson reveals about student thinking such as their misconceptions, difficulties, confusion, insights, and surprising ideas;
- how the lesson was designed and/or studied; and
- the practice of teaching and learning in your field.

Recommend any further revisions to the lesson and discuss any remaining questions or concerns.

References

List any theoretical, empirical, or pedagogical sources that you consulted or cited in your lesson study. Use a documentation style appropriate to your discipline or field (e.g., APA for psychology and MLA for English).

Appendix

Include

- materials used to teach the lesson including student handouts and instructor's notes. Please annotate each item with a brief description.
- materials used to study the lesson including observation guidelines, written questions, prompts, and checklists. Please annotate each item with a brief description.
- evidence and data not included in the text of the report such as observers' notes, examples of student work, and data analysis results.

Appendix 7.B:
Teaching Improvement Profile

The Teaching Improvement Profile (TIP) is intended for individual instructors who want to document their lesson study work for purposes of retention, promotion, and tenure decisions. The audiences for the TIP will be departmental colleagues and members of one's institutional review committees. Instructors can adapt the TIP contents to best fit their institutional requirements.

The template below begins with a short TIP description and its relation to lesson study. This is intended for external readers who are not familiar with lesson study practices. The template includes eight sections: (a) Introduction, (b) background context, (c) student learning goals, (d) lesson design, (e) rationale for lesson design, (f) analysis of the lesson, (g) reflection, and (h) appendix with supporting materials.

Several of the template's sections include prompts, actual sentences and paragraphs that instructors can use to structure their responses if they choose to do so. The words in italics in brackets are suggestions about what information to include in the profile.

This TIP explains my lesson study experience during [*indicate time period*]. Student handouts and other pertinent materials are attached in the appendix.

INTRODUCTION

In this section

1. *describe lesson study briefly;*
2. *indicate your time commitment during the academic year and describe what you did in general terms; and*

3. *refer to completed work or work in progress (e.g., Final Lesson Study Report, article for publication).*

During [*time frame*] I participated in lesson study with [*names of team members*]. Our group met [*number of meetings*] for a total of [*number of hours*] in fall and spring semester. In the first semester we designed and taught the lesson, collected evidence of student learning, and used the evidence to revise the lesson. The second semester we repeated this cycle by teaching and observing the revised lesson, collecting additional evidence of student learning, and revising the lesson a second time.

We completed a Final Lesson Study Report, which documents the lesson study in greater depth. A copy of the report is in the appendix. [*Or*] Currently our group is working on a Final Lesson Study Report that will document the lesson study in greater depth and detail.

BACKGROUND CONTEXT

In this section

1. *describe the course and the lesson study topic; and*
2. *explain the rationale for selecting the topic (e.g., it's a particularly difficult topic for students; it's a new area of the curriculum).*

The course [*include a brief description and relevant information—number of students, why they take it, etc.*]

We developed a research lesson on the topic of (*specify topic*). We chose this topic because [*provide a reason for choosing this topic*].

The rationale will be more compelling if you characterize the lesson as a potential solution to a learning problem—e.g., students do not understand X, Y, or Z. It will be even more compelling if you can document the nature of the problem with observations, data, or indicate it is a well-known student learning problem in your field.

STUDENT LEARNING GOALS

In this section

1. *describe the lesson's short- and long-term learning goals. State these in terms of the knowledge, skills, abilities, values, and dispositions students should develop as a result of the lesson;*

2. *acknowledge that a single lesson cannot fully develop larger long-term goals but that it can make a contribution to their development; and*

3. *point out any connections between the lesson's goals and departmental goals and objectives.*

The lesson is designed to foster short- and long-term learning goals. As a result of the lesson students should be able to/better able to [*give a broad idea of what students should achieve through the lesson*]. A single lesson cannot fully develop these long-term [*identify the long-term capacities, skills, attitudes, dispositions*]. However, it is important to address these in individual classes.

LESSON DESIGN

In this section

1. *include a* summary *of the lesson plan with the approximate amount of time necessary for each segment. Include a detailed lesson plan in the appendix;*

2. *indicate who does what—e.g., The instructor explained . . . or Students worked in small groups on . . . (This helps the reader get a better sense of the lesson as a teaching and learning episode.); and*

3. *refer to handouts and relevant materials and include them in the appendix.*

RATIONALE FOR LESSON DESIGN

In this section, explain the rationale for the lesson design—how and why do the specific instructional and learning activities support the desired changes in student learning and thinking?

The rationale should explain the relationship between teaching and learning and should focus on how students learn from the specific activities and exercises. The following examples illustrate progressively more specific and substantive explanations of student learning.

1. *Students worked in groups for part of the lesson. We chose group work because it actively involves students in learning. Students who are active are more likely to learn the material. (Generic—active learning is a good thing.)*

2. *Students worked in groups for part of the lesson. The group task was designed so that students would apply course concepts to new problems. Students had the opportunity to think about how the material applies in "real-life" contexts and not just as textbook information to memorize. They are more likely to think about the meaning of the ideas and not simply memorize the information. (More specific—the rationale appeals to "application" as a way to foster understanding.)*

3. *Students worked in groups for part of the lesson. The group task was designed so that students used course material to explain several novel examples. Members of the group were obliged to give feedback and suggestions about how to strengthen one another's explanations. We chose this task because developing an explanation involves students in trying to make sense of the material and establish relevant connections among ideas. Further, feedback from other students would, if nothing else, get students to question their understanding of the topic. (More fully developed—the rationale indicates that "explanation" is a sense-making activity and that feedback can prompt students to question their level of understanding. These activities can be observed and analyzed during the lesson.)*

ANALYSIS OF THE LESSON

In this section

1. *Describe the types of evidence of student learning you collected including (a) observations of student learning and thinking during the lesson and (b) evaluation of student learning before and/or after the lesson.*

2. *Summarize the results in terms of what students learned (based on any pre- and postlesson evidence) and how they learned or did not learn what was taught (based on observational evidence from the lesson).*

3. *Explain the results. Based on the evidence, how did the lesson support (and not support) achievement of the learning goals. Explain other "interesting" findings even if they are not directly related to the lesson goals. Discuss the significance of the results and what they mean for improving the lesson.*

REFLECTION

In this section, tell the reader what you have learned from lesson study and how it has affected your classroom instruction and/or pedagogical thinking. Cite specific examples to illustrate changes in your practices or thinking.

The following are possible prompts:

1. *Why did you become involved in lesson study? What are your teaching improvement goals?*
2. *Discuss specific insights about student learning that came out of the lesson study.*
3. *Discuss ways your teaching has changed or has begun to change in terms of class planning, goal setting, classroom practices, assessment of student learning, use of assessment to improve teaching and learning, and your understanding of how students learn the subject you teach.*

Appendix 7.C:
Teaching Improvement Profile Example

Bill Cerbin, May 2005 [2005a]

What Is a Teaching Improvement Profile?

Teaching, "like other forms of scholarship, is an extended process that unfolds over time. It embodies at least five elements: vision, design, interactions, outcomes, and analysis" (Shulman, 1998).

1. Vision: the instructor's goals that specify what students should learn and develop.
2. Design: the design of assignments, exercises, and experiences intended to make the goals come to life.
3. Interactions: the enactment of teaching and learning in the classroom, engaging students with the subject matter through discussion, lecturing, problem solving, collaborative work, exercises, and assignments.
4. Outcomes: the acts and products of student learning consisting of changes in understanding, skills, competencies, propensities, and sensibilities.
5. Analysis: the interpretation and analysis of how and how well students learn from the experience.

Lesson Study is a teaching improvement process in which a small group of instructors jointly designs, teaches, observes, evaluates, and revises a single class lesson—called a Research Lesson (Lewis & Tsuchida, 1998b; Stigler & Hiebert, 1999). Because it embodies all five elements of teaching—vision, design, interactions, outcomes, and analysis—lesson study is an ideal context in which to document teaching improvement. This Teaching Improvement Profile provides evidence and analysis of, and reflection on, lesson study activities.

Lewis, C., & Tsuchida, I. (1998b). A lesson is like a swiftly flowing river. *American Educator, 22*(4), 12–17; 50–52.

Stigler, J. W., & Hiebert, J. (1999). *The teaching gap: Best ideas from the world's teachers for improving education in the classroom.* New York, NY: Free Press.

Shulman, L. (1998). Course anatomy: The dissection and analysis of knowledge through teaching. In P. Hutchings (Ed.), *The course portfolio: How faculty can examine their teaching to advance practice and improve student learning.* Washington, DC: American Association for Higher Education.

This TIP explains my lesson study experience during 2003–2004. Student handouts and other pertinent materials are attached in the appendix.

INTRODUCTION

During 2003–2004 I participated in lesson study with Melanie Cary, Rob Dixon, and Carmen Wilson. In fall semester we designed, taught, observed, evaluated, and revised a research lesson on Bystander Intervention in my introductory psychology class. Spring semester we repeated the cycle and revised the lesson a second time. We met about 11 times for a total of 25–30 hours during the year. Our final Research Lesson Report documents the lesson study in greater depth. A copy is in the appendix and online at http://www.uwlax.edu/sotl/lsp/gallery.htm.

BACKGROUND CONTEXT

Introductory Psychology addresses major topics and themes in psychology. It is a required first course in the undergraduate major and also meets a general education requirement. Both semesters the class enrolled 30 first-year students. About half the students had a high school psychology class but they were not familiar with the topic of Bystander Intervention. I taught the research lesson both times, November 2003 and April 2004. Melanie, Carmen, and Rob observed the lesson on both occasions.

The research lesson topic, "Bystander Intervention: Why Onlookers Come to the Aid of Strangers in Need of Help," is the first lesson in a section on social psychology. We chose bystander intervention because the research on bystander behavior tends to conflict with popular beliefs about why strangers help or do not help. It seemed an interesting way to get students thinking about how and why the presence of other people in a situation influences individual behavior.

STUDENT LEARNING GOALS

As a result of the lesson students should

1. be able to explain the "bystander effect," i.e., that the presence of onlookers decreases the chances that an individual bystander will assist a stranger in need of help;
2. be able to explain how the presence of other people influences bystander behavior; and
3. be better able to analyze and explain human behavior in terms of relationships among multiple factors (or variables).

The first and second goals are specific to the lesson. The third is a course goal and, more broadly, a goal for the undergraduate psychology major. Psychological reasoning involves thinking in terms of the relationships among variables. To explain any form of behavior, we need to determine the factors, conditions, variables, and antecedents that influence the actions in question. Most people engage in this kind of thinking on a daily basis and gradually develop "intuitive theories" to explain what makes people tick. In the general psychology course we introduce students to many psychological models on a wide range of topics. They are good at remembering the models but have trouble using them to explain and predict human behavior. Moreover, their own "intuitive theories" of behavior tend to interfere with learning and using discipline-based models. Consequently, an important course goal is to help students move beyond commonsense explanations and develop an understanding of empirically tested models of human behavior.

LESSON DESIGN

Before class. One week before the lesson, students took a Bystander Intervention Pretest consisting of seven scenarios depicting people in need of assistance. They predicted whether bystanders would help or not help in the situations, and what factors would influence bystanders' behavior.

During class (85-minute class period)

- I described the lesson and gave written directions to students (5 minutes).
- I divided the class for group work (40 minutes)
  - In small groups students created a list of factors that influence bystander intervention.
  - I circulated among groups to answer questions.
  - Students prepared a written summary and an overhead transparency with their group's list of factors.
- I led a class discussion, asking students to explain their factors and compare them to those of other groups. I then introduced the research-based model of bystander intervention (20 minutes).
- Students analyzed their factors against the research-based bystander intervention model (10 minutes).
- Students wrote an individual analysis of how their group's factors fit or did not fit the bystander model (5 minutes).

After class. Students completed a Bystander Intervention Posttest in which they predicted bystander behavior in four scenarios. At the next class period I led a class discussion comparing students' posttest answers to the actual research results.

RATIONALE FOR LESSON DESIGN

Rather than tell students about bystander intervention (lecture), we decided to involve them in analyzing and explaining bystander behavior in terms of relationships among variables. I believe students are more likely to understand the multifactorial nature of behavior if they generate and test their own models of behavior against research-based models. Moreover, we are aware that students hold a common misconception about helping behavior (i.e., "good people help, bad people don't"). I think they are more likely to revise their beliefs if they confront the incongruities directly.

As the lesson progressed there were three opportunities to revise and extend their understanding of this form of social behavior: (a) individually producing factors that influence bystanders to help or not to help (pretest), (b) comparing their explanations of bystander intervention to the research-based model of bystander intervention (group work in class), and (c) predicting and explaining how bystanders would act in several novel situations (posttest).

ANALYSIS OF THE LESSON

Types of evidence of student learning:

1. *Observations of students.* Three members of the lesson study team attended the class. Each instructor observed a single small group and recorded field notes throughout the lesson.
2. *Written analyses.* Students wrote individual analyses at the end of the class period. These were used to evaluate their grasp of the research model.
3. *Pre- and posttests.* Bystander Intervention pre- and posttests were used to evaluate students' understanding of the factors that influence bystander intervention.

Students' understanding changed in three areas:

1. *Understanding diffusion of responsibility.* Prior to the lesson students tended to think a bystander is more likely to help when other bystanders are present in a situation (i.e., "strength in numbers"). On the posttest a large majority of students indicated that help is less likely when other bystanders are present, based on the idea of "diffusion of responsibility."
2. *Understanding how social context affects individual behavior.* On the pretest 87% of students based their predictions, at least in part, on the bystander's character (e.g., empathic and caring bystanders are more likely to help than those who lack empathy and do not care what happens to other people). On the posttest, however, only 17% of students referred to the bystander's personality or disposition. But, observations during the lesson indicated that some students remained ambivalent about the importance of the bystander's "character." For example, one student said something to the effect that "I still believe that if you are a certain kind of person you will help out regardless of how many people are around."
3. *Understanding relationships among variables.* On the posttest students were better able to state causal connections between factors in the situation (e.g., number of bystanders) and subsequent behavior (i.e., whether a person would help or not). The lesson helped develop students' ability to analyze and explain human behavior in terms of relationships among multiple variables.

REFLECTION

The research lesson was relatively successful and stands on its own as evidence of teaching improvement. Additionally, we have field-tested the lesson twice and can make evidence-based claims about its strengths as well as shortcomings.

The purpose of lesson study is not to create exemplary lessons but to develop a way to analyze and improve teaching and learning. Because lesson study involves scholarly inquiry into student learning, it can be not only a way to improve the teaching of those who participate in it but also a way to advance the practice of teaching more generally. I view it as a way to improve my teaching practices and contribute to pedagogical knowledge in my field.

What I am learning, thinking, and doing as a result of lesson study.

The importance of learning goals. I am a proponent of backward design—the idea that you articulate what you want students to accomplish first and then design instruction to address those goals. This sounds good in theory but it is hard to do in practice. In the lesson study process we stayed true to our learning goals, which provided a clear focus and purpose for the design of the lesson. It is especially challenging to think about how a single lesson contributes to larger, long-term goals. Looking at how a lesson supports student development in a broader sense altered my view of a lesson itself. Rather than an independent learning episode, a lesson should be part of a larger whole, linked in a purposeful way to other lessons that support cumulative learning and long-term development of important values, dispositions and abilities.

Purposeful instructional design. I always prepare for class, but not in ways that would best support student learning. In the design of our research lesson it has been valuable to make explicit the rationale for lesson design, to think about how certain strategies, exercises, and experiences facilitate and support changes in student thinking. For example, our group developed bystander scenarios depicting situations in which a person needed assistance. These enabled us to evaluate student beliefs and understanding of bystander intervention in a systematic way. These were also important teaching tools that engaged students in thinking about multiple causes of behavior—just the kind of thinking the lesson was intended to develop.

It is impossible to plan and design each lesson like a research lesson; however, as I continue to do lesson study I expect to find better ways to support specific learning goals.

Making student thinking visible. I view learning as inherently problematic, and lesson study is a way to develop a better understanding of how and why students learn or do not learn what they are taught. To study a lesson you need to make students' thinking visible and open to observation and analysis. I believe this is one of the most important pedagogical features of lesson study because it enables teachers to watch as students attempt to make sense of the subject matter and to observe the changes in their thinking that take place during the lesson. This is like opening a window into the minds of students at just the right time—when they are responding to the lesson. Our research lesson was moderately successful in this regard, but I think we still missed important features of the learning process. I am very interested in developing better ways to make student thinking visible that are, simultaneously, significant learning opportunities. For example, in Japanese lessons students are repeatedly asked to explain their reasoning and thinking during a lesson. This reveals how they construe the subject. At the same time, the act of explaning is an important way to make sense of material and develop one's understanding of it. Tapping into students' thinking during the lesson provides the "data" instructors need to decide how to make the lesson more effective.

The Practice and Potential
of Lesson Study

Starting at the base level of "What do students know?" and "What do they bring with them?" helped cultivate for me a stronger sense of, in some ways, empathy and perspective in my teaching. Rather than thinking about the students I wish I had or I speculate I have, SoTL of all sorts and lesson study in particular helps me to address the students I actually have, what they know, and how to meet them where they are. One outcome of our lesson study on introducing students to the discipline of literary studies helped us to realize the kinds of misconceptions that students bring with them to the study of literature. This is a tremendous realization both for me personally and, I believe, for our discipline in thinking about the teaching of literature and how to address those misunderstandings that students bring with them to the classroom. (English Instructor)

Lesson study is in its infancy in higher education. Consequently, little is known about what college teachers experience during a lesson study and how they benefit from it. As part of their participation in the College Lesson Study Project, instructors are asked to report on their experience. They complete two questionnaires, the first at the midpoint and the second at the end of their lesson study. In the Mid-Year Questionnaire, participants discuss their initial experience and rate the relative difficulty of various lesson study processes. At the end of the lesson study instructors complete a Lesson Study Experiences Questionnaire in which they reflect on a broad range of topics. Based on these findings, we are starting to understand what college lesson studies look like in practice and how participation in lesson study affects teachers and teaching (Cerbin, 2008).

INITIAL LESSON STUDY EXPERIENCE

The purpose of the Mid-Year Questionnaire is to assess instructors' experiences early in the lesson study experience and to identify specific activities in which they had difficulty. Table 8.1 reports the difficulty ratings for various lesson study activities.

As indicated in the table, about two-thirds of the respondents thought that teaching and observing the research lesson and working as a team were not difficult activities. In contrast, *making student thinking visible, designing data collection strategies,* and *analyzing evidence* were viewed as difficult by more than 75% of the instructors. Overall, these data suggest that activities associated with teaching (e.g., lesson planning and teaching the research lesson) were relatively easy for teams to accomplish and those related to studying the lesson were significantly more difficult. These are not surprising results given that few instructors engage in classroom research. In fact, for many participants lesson study is their first experience performing systematic classroom inquiry. The results also indicate that the first iteration of lesson study involves learning how to carry out the process. As one mathematics instructor said, "I had often read about lesson study, but before you experience the process, you lack real understanding of the process." And, as instructors discover, the process is intellectually challenging.

STICKING POINTS: WHAT IS DIFFICULT ABOUT DOING LESSON STUDY?

Lesson study is a mixture of the familiar and the new. Preparing for and teaching class are routine activities, but setting goals, implementing backward design, and making student thinking visible introduce new challenges.

Table 8.1   Instructors' Ratings of Lesson Study Activities

Lesson Study Activity	Not Difficult (%)	Moderately Difficult (%)	Very Difficult (%)
Developing learning goals	36.98	60.27	2.70
Designing lesson activities	33.33	63.89	2.70
Making student thinking visible	16.43	65.75	17.80
Designing data collection strategies	23.60	62.50	13.88
Teaching the lesson	65.15	33.33	1.50
Observing student learning	67.19	29.69	3.10
Analyzing evidence	25.00	60.00	15.00
Using evidence to revise lesson	33.89	57.63	8.40
Working as a team	62.31	27.54	10.15

Below are comments from instructors about specific aspects of the process they found difficult in the early phase of lesson study.

Learning goals
- Switching perspectives from teaching goals to learning goals
- Trying to state abstract goals in terms of concrete actions
- Trying to address broad developmental goals in a single lesson

Backward design
- The novelty of starting with a goal and then thinking of how to teach to it
- Trying to explain how an instructional activity actually supports student thinking

Making student thinking visible
- This is hard in a large class where student interaction is limited.
- Difficult to come up with techniques that promote learning

Analyzing evidence
- Challenging to sort and organize so much information
- Tough to decide what is most important in all the evidence
- Using evidence to revise the lesson
- Too many things to change
- Trying to decide what change would make the most difference for student learning

These comments reflect substantive—but not insurmountable—challenges. Like any novice, an instructor gets better at the process with practice. One good reason to do a second iteration of lesson study is so that participants have an opportunity to improve their own inquiry skills—that is, to get better at doing lesson study.

HOW LESSON STUDY AFFECTS TEACHERS AND THEIR TEACHING PRACTICES

At the completion of their lesson study, teachers reflected on how their lesson study experiences influenced their (a) pedagogical thinking, (b) teaching practices, (c) understanding of students, (d) collaboration with colleagues, and (e) understanding of the subject matter (see the Lesson Study Experiences Questionnaire in Appendix 8.A). The results indicate that lesson study has wide-ranging effects on instructors. Most respondents cited several ways that the experience influenced their pedagogical thinking, their knowledge of students, and their teaching practices. The most common themes are discussed below.

Instructors view the following aspects of the experience as especially significant and beneficial:

- Collaborating with colleagues
- Examining alternative ways to teach
- Observing and analyzing student learning

One of the most frequent themes was the importance of collaborating with colleagues. Instructors talked about how much they appreciated and learned from working with fellow teachers. Many indicated that lesson study was the first time they had worked closely with other instructors to focus on teaching issues.

One psychology instructor pointed out the benefits of collaboration:

What I liked about lesson study was collaborating with my teaching colleagues in a formal way on improving a lesson we all taught. I got to see my colleagues' approaches to the same topic and also their perceptions and approaches about problems in teaching the topic. I liked that we developed a shared lesson that integrated our different perspectives and approaches. Most of my past experience with discussing teaching issues with my colleagues has mostly occurred informally as discussions around the lunchroom table or even at faculty department meetings. But lesson study required us to come to a consensus on how we were going to teach the lesson.

A communications instructor reflected on how the experience resulted in a valuable form of peer mentoring:

For me, as a new instructor, this experience helped me to understand the topic we chose much more, which helped me to teach it better. It also developed a close bond between my two partners and me. This bond has resulted in a professional relationship where I feel I can go to either one of them for help on anything. This sharing of ideas among colleagues is not something that is part of our department.

An instructor of risk control pointed out the benefits of learning by doing:

We all agreed that we liked to collaborate together and that we really appreciated being able to collaborate in a nonthreatening, team-oriented way. In a way, I came to realize that we, as teachers, need to learn about teaching the same way that our students learn best—by doing rather than sitting in a lecture. Lesson study is a very useful tool to have teachers learning by doing.

They also noted that lesson study involves sustained long-term collaboration focused on specific teaching and learning problems. In this sense, lesson study promotes the kind of collaboration that is typical of research teams that work on problems over a long period of time. Instructors note that sharing their ideas with teammates enriches their understanding of teaching. They have substantive conversations about teaching and discuss alternative ways to teach. Instructors find it valuable to hear how their colleagues approach teaching the same topics. Participants start to view their colleagues as important resources and collaborators, and indicate they would be interested in working with them on future teaching projects.

Instructors underscored the significance of observing and analyzing student learning. They commented on how this changed their perspective of what takes place in class. For most, it was the first time they had observed firsthand the interplay between instruction and students' reactions. Some indicated that seeing students externalize misconceptions or revise their thinking gave them a new appreciation for the difficulty of learning their subject matter. A mathematics instructor noted,

Observing a colleague and her classes while she was teaching the lesson helped me focus more on student understanding of both process and concepts . . . since I now had this opportunity to directly observe what students were doing and saying in small groups.

Influence on Pedagogical Thinking

The Lesson Study Experiences Questionnaire asks instructors to cite any changes in their assumptions and beliefs about teaching. The following selection of responses indicates that some instructors shift their views or start to look at teaching differently as a result of lesson study participation:

- *Just because you're teaching doesn't mean students are learning.*
- *Instructors need to see classes as students see them.*
- *Shift from my experience to what students are getting from the class*
- *The emphasis on making student thinking visible*
- *For the first time I understand what true assessment looks like.*
- *Orienting teaching around learning goals and not just covering material*

As these comments suggest, instructors focused on how they achieved greater awareness of student learning and the importance of trying to see the subject and the class from students' perspectives. In recent years, educators have promoted the idea of being student-centered or learning-centered. Because lesson study focuses on how students learn, it can be a way to support the development of learning-centered instruction. At the very least, teachers come away from the experience with a heightened awareness of what instruction looks like from their students' perspective.

An English instructor talked about understanding the topic better as a result of contemplating how to teach it to novice students:

> *Putting the subject matter under a microscope in some ways helped me to understand it better, at least in articulating consciously what the values of my field are and what I hope students will leave the class with. Thinking about where students go wrong in approaching literature certainly helped me understand the challenges in my field that perhaps I didn't always have but hadn't thought hard enough about.*

A political science instructor talked about taking students' point of view:

> *We had to put ourselves in the role of students, challenge our assumptions about what they thought about citizenship.*

A history instructor reflected on planning changes:

> *I need to pare down my lesson plans. I try to do too much and the students get confused. My lectures get too long and I run out of time to do the active learning portion. I really need to be conscious to just give a 15- to 20-minute introduction, then let the students play with the primary sources and come to their own conclusion.*

A mathematics instructor talked about using goals to plan classes:

> *It definitely reminded me that I often focus too much on "covering the material" rather than focusing on student learning. It gave me a new appreciation of thinking seriously about course goals, and teaching with those in mind.*

Influence on Teaching Practices

When asked to describe how lesson study influenced their actual teaching practices instructors cited many specific examples related to how they would teach the research lesson topic differently than they had in the past. More general themes that emerged included

- taking more risks, trying alternative methods;
- using learning goals to plan classes; and
- believing the class period should have a "point."

Instructors indicated that they were more willing to try out different teaching approaches. They used the phrase *take more risks* to indicate they planned to try alternative practices in their classes. Another recurring theme was the importance of using learning goals as the basis for planning class. Teachers did not explicitly talk about using backward design, but they started to think more about what students should get out of a class when they prepared for class. Some went so far as to say that each class period should have a point, in terms of what students should know or be able to do as a result of daily class lessons.

Because of lesson study, a political science instructor gained confidence in teaching:

When I started teaching, it was very teacher-oriented, but now I increasingly rely on techniques to push students to participate in their own education and to do work on their own (with my guidance of course and with the set of resources/instructions). I also increasingly look at originality of thinking, analysis, and synthesis, not just reiteration of facts, even in lower-division classes. In all my classes I have significant hands-on elements and I also try to have more student discussions in all my classes. This is not necessarily [a] new idea to me, but I learned to trust students much more through the lesson-study experience.

An English instructor talked about the significance of goal setting:

Lesson study helped me make more explicit my goals for my literature courses. In some sense this is what I have always been grasping at throughout graduate school and in my early career, a way to make explicit and concrete the goals for literary studies and what I hope my students will leave their courses with, what abilities I want them to have cognitively/intellectually. It has helped me, especially collaborating with some respected colleagues, [to] articulate that more clearly and [to] design instruction specifically geared toward accomplishing that learning outcome.

A psychology instructor talked about shifting orientations from content coverage to student engagement and learning:

I have changed a lot about my courses to allow for more student participation, more student-directed work, and more course-work interaction. Coverage is no longer my sole concern. Rather, I am as concerned about student engagement and student connection to the University in general.

Influence on Understanding of Students

Instructors talked about how lesson study had led to better understanding of

- how students construe the subject matter;
- how students interpret and experience the instructional activities in class; and
- students' capacities and limitations.

Japanese teachers often refer to lesson study as a way to see the subject through their students' eyes. College instructors also describe how observing students gives them insight into how students interpret and make sense of the topic. Teachers also say they learn more about how students experience the lesson itself. For example, instructors who observed students working in small groups commented on how it was the first time they had really watched students engage in interactive learning. They observed students who were off task, confused, or interacting in ineffective ways, or how students supported one another's learning, engaged in the topic with enthusiasm, etc.

A physics instructor described the importance of seeing student thinking in situ:

It helped us confirm that students really lack conceptual understanding of simple concepts like pressure; seeing that in the study, rather than seeing [it] in some report, made a difference in my thinking about how difficult it is for students to master concepts in physics.

A statistics instructor discovered how students approach certain problems:

I didn't realize how dependent the classification of a type of probability was on the way a problem is approached. Many probability scenarios have events that can be classified as any of the three types of probability depending on what information is available and what information the student may assume he has access to.

A library instructor said,

I found that in the library lesson, for example, we needed to start with far more basics, and proceed much more slowly than I [had] thought. A step-by-step process of searching for research materials was necessary.

Another library instructor commented,

> *Because of the way that we designed the . . . lesson, with mini-lectures followed by several segments where the students work on questions on a worksheet, I can for the first time observe the impact of my instruction and see what problem areas there are in understanding how to use the library. It is brilliant and I love it. I have a much better understanding of what the students have learned.*

These preliminary findings show that with minimal training, college teachers engage in substantive lesson study practices. Instructors report that they revise their thinking about teaching, learn alternative ways to teach their subject, and gain a deeper understanding of how their students learn from instruction. Of course, much more research is needed before we understand how participation in lesson study, especially long-term participation, affects teaching and learning.

Appendix 8.A:
Lesson Study Experience Questionnaire

Introduction. This questionnaire is for lesson study grant recipients who have completed one or more lesson studies. It focuses on your involvement in lesson study and how the experience has influenced you. This is the first study that explores how participation in lesson study affects college instructors and I sincerely appreciate your contribution to this effort.

Your participation in this questionnaire is voluntary. By completing it you are granting permission to me to use your responses for research purposes. Your responses will be kept anonymous. Excerpts of responses may be used in presentations or publications, but your name will not be associated with individual responses.

Please send the completed questionnaire to:

Background information

Institution: Discipline:

Current rank: Tenured; not tenured; not in a
                                                                tenure line position

Years of college teaching experience: Male/Female:

1. Estimate the total number of hours your team met during your lesson study:

2. How many lesson studies have you participated in (Note: A single lesson study refers to the study of one lesson regardless of how many times you revise, teach, and study that lesson)?

3. Are you currently involved in a lesson study?

4. If not currently involved, when were you last involved in a lesson study?

5. How did you learn to do lesson study? Check all that apply.
   ____ Participated in a lesson study training workshop
   ____ Attended a conference presentation about lesson study
   ____ Completed one or more PowerPoint lesson study training modules
   ____ Read and watched the multimedia online guide on the lesson study website
   ____ Read the training manual, *Using Lesson Study to Improve Teaching & Learning*
   ____ Watched Japanese video, *Can You Lift 100kg?*
   ____ Watched DVD video, *Introduction to Lesson Study*
   ____ Used materials from the College Lesson Study website
   ____ Used materials from the College Lesson Study blog
   ____ Read examples of lesson study teams' final reports
   ____ Read articles about lesson study in K–12 education
   ____ Participated in a lesson study team with colleagues who already knew how to do lesson study and who "showed me the ropes."
   ____ Other: please describe
   ____ No training

6. How often were you an *active participant* on your team?
   ____ Frequently __ Sometimes __ Seldom __ Never

7. Were you your team's leader (e.g., contact person for grant)?
   __ Yes __ No

8. To what extent do you feel like you are a *co-author* of your team's research lesson?
   __ Very much so __ To some extent __ A little __ Not at all

9. To what extent do you feel like you are a *co-author* of your team's final report?
   __ Very much so __ To some extent __ A little __ Not at all

10. How effective is lesson study as a way to improve teaching?
    __ Very effective __ Somewhat effective
    __ Somewhat ineffective __ Very ineffective

11. How effective is lesson study as a way to do the scholarship of teaching and learning?
    __ Very effective __ Somewhat effective
    __ Somewhat ineffective __ Very ineffective

12. How would you rate your overall lesson study experience?
    __ Very positive __ Somewhat positive __ Neutral
    __ Somewhat negative __ Very negative

13. Under the right circumstances would you participate in lesson study again in the future?
    __ Yes __ No

    If you answered yes, please describe the *right circumstances.*

The final three open-ended questions ask you to write your lesson study experiences. They focus on what was worthwhile, beneficial, or negative, and whether involvement in lesson study has influenced your teaching and your views on teaching and learning. Please give specific examples whenever possible.

---

14. Comment on your lesson study experience. Emphasize and explain any features you think were particularly significant, worthwhile, beneficial, or negative.

15. This section asks you to reflect on ways that lesson study has *influenced* your attitudes, thinking, and behavior. *Influence* has a broad meaning. For example, it can refer to how your lesson study experience stimulated your thinking about some aspect of teaching, led to some realization about students, or changed the way you actually teach.

The questions in the following table are intended to prompt your thinking— you do not need to respond to each one. Please give specific examples whenever possible.

In what ways, if any, did your lesson study experience influence your ***thinking about teaching and learning*?** Consider things like • your attitudes toward teaching, students • your philosophy, vision, beliefs, assumptions about teaching and learning • your sense of being able to affect student learning or improve instruction • any epiphanies • anything else related to thinking	In what ways, if any, did your lesson study experience influence your ***teaching practices*?** Consider things like • how you organize and plan classes • how you prepare instructional materials • instructional strategies or techniques you use • how you evaluate student learning • anything else related to teaching practices	In what ways, if any, did your lesson study experience influence your ***understanding of students*?** Consider things like • your understanding of student learning and thinking • how you observe and interact with students in your classes • ways you take student learning and thinking into account in your teaching • anything else related to students
In what ways, if any, did your lesson study experience influence your ***collaboration with colleagues*?** Consider things like • your attitude about collaboration with colleagues • the quality of interactions with colleagues • anything else related to collaboration	In what ways, if any, did your lesson study experience influence your ***understanding of the subject matter*** related to the lesson?	Describe **any other ways** that involvement in lesson study has influenced you.

16. Please offer suggestions or advice about how to improve any aspect of the Lesson Study Project.

Epilogue

In higher education the pathways to becoming a good teacher are not well marked. Even though teaching is intellectually demanding and complex work, most college instructors have no formal training that prepares them to teach. Largely, we learn how to teach on the job—from our own teaching experiences.

Experience alone does not guarantee that we will improve. We can do something repeatedly for a long period of time—acquire a lot of experience—but not improve at it. So, how do we get better at teaching? How do we become expert teachers?

Research shows that *deliberate practice* is essential to develop expertise. Unlike simple experience, deliberate practice is a structured activity intended to improve performance. It focuses on specific parts of complex performance and involves extensive feedback to improve future effort (Ericsson, Krampe, & Tesch-Romer, 1993). Extensive research with experts in many different fields demonstrates that high-level expertise develops only as a result of many years of deliberate practice.

> A number of researchers have endorsed what has become known as the "ten-year-rule": one can't become an expert in any field in less than ten years, be it physics, chess, golf, or mathematics. This rule has been applied to fields as diverse as musical composition, mathematics, poetry, competitive swimming, and car sales. (Willingham, 2009, p. 107)

If we aspire to improve our practice and become expert teachers, we should think seriously about what constitutes deliberate practice and how to make it part of our work. Certainly, many college teachers participate in professional and instructional development activities, participate in teaching workshops, and read articles about teaching and learning. Teachers also make changes intended to improve their classes (e.g., revise tests or develop new assignments). These may be valuable experiences but typically do not constitute deliberate practice. Attending a workshop or reading about a new teaching approach is not the same as implementing the approach, practicing, receiving feedback, and then improving it.

. However, we have seen that lesson study involves deliberate practice. Furthermore, it entails practice of the entire teaching and learning process—formulating goals, identifying and analyzing student learning problems, designing instructional materials and activities, teaching a lesson, observing and analyzing student learning, collecting evidence of student performance, and using evidence to improve teaching and learning.

A single lesson study does not create master teachers. But instructors could adopt lesson study practices as a strategy to improve their teaching and address important goals and priorities in their programs. Imagine these types of scenarios:

- Several instructors use lesson study each year to investigate student learning in a large, multisection survey course. Over time, lesson study becomes the primary means by which instructors improve their teaching and also improve the course.
- Instructors do lesson studies in three courses (introductory, intermediate, and upper level) to examine student learning with respect to a key learning goal in the program. They use the results to supplement their departmental assessment activities.
- New instructors are invited to join a lesson study group in their first year as a way to become oriented to teaching in the program.
- Several instructors who plan to adopt a new teaching strategy do a lesson study to explore how it works in practice.
- Instructors plan several lesson studies to examine a persistent learning gap in which a disproportionate number of students have difficulty making the transition from sophomore- to junior-level courses.

Each lesson study is an opportunity to work on improving teaching and learning and also address additional goals such as mentoring new faculty, performing departmental assessment, implementing and evaluating new teaching strategies, and systematically improving an important course in the curriculum.

I hope that as more college teachers experiment with lesson study, it will gradually be adopted as a tool to improve individual teaching and used collectively to advance the practice of teaching and learning more broadly.

References

Angelo, T., & Cross, K. P. (1993). *Classroom assessment techniques: A handbook for college teachers* (2nd ed.). San Francisco, CA: Jossey-Bass.

Barkley, E., Cross, K. P., & Major, C. (2005). *Collaborative learning techniques: A handbook for college faculty.* San Francisco, CA: Jossey-Bass.

Bartell, D., Furlong, S., Gurung, R., Kersten, A., & Wilson-Doenges, G. (2007, March). An interdisciplinary lesson plan to foster student engagement. *Teaching Forum: A Journal of the Scholarship of Teaching and Learning (Special Issue: Using Lesson Study to Advance Teaching and Learning).* Retrieved from http://www.uwlax.edu/teachingforum/index.html

Becker, J., Ghenciu P., Horak, M., & Schroeder, H. (2008). A college lesson study in calculus, preliminary report. *International Journal of Mathematical Education in Science and Technology, 39*(4), 491–503.

Bloom, B., Engelhart, M., Furst, E., Hill, W., & Krathwohl, D. (1956). *Taxonomy of educational objectives: The classification of educational goals; Handbook I: Cognitive domain.* Susan Fauer Company. New York: Longmans, Green.

Bradley Commission on History in Schools, (1995). *Building a history curriculum: Guidelines for teaching history in schools.* Westlake, OH: National Council for History Education.

Bransford, J., Brown, A., & Cocking, R. (2005). *How students learn: History, mathematics, and science in the classroom.* Washington, DC: National Academies Press.

Bransford, J., & Schwartz, D. (1999). Re-thinking transfer: A simple proposal with multiple implications. *Review of Research in Education, 24*(40), 61–100.

Broudy, H. (1977). Types of knowledge and purposes of education. In R. C. Anderson, R. J. Spiro, & W. E. Montague (Eds.), *Schooling and the acquisition of knowledge.* Hillsdale, NJ: Lawrence Erlbaum Associates.

Carver, S. (2006). Assessing for deep understanding. In K. Sawyer (Ed.), *The Cambridge handbook of the learning sciences.* Cambridge: Cambridge University Press.

Cerbin, B. (2005a). Teaching improvement profile example. Retrieved from http://www.uwlax.edu/sotl/lsp/templates/tipexample.pdf

Cerbin, B. (2005b). Teaching improvement profile template (TIP). Retrieved from http://www.uwlax.edu/sotl/lsp/templates/teachingimprovementprofile.pdf

Cerbin, B. (2007, March). A note from the guest editor: What is a lesson study? *Teaching Forum: A Journal of the Scholarship of Teaching and Learning (Special*

Issue: Using Lesson Study to Advance Teaching and Learning). Retrieved from http://www.uwlax.edu/teachingforum/index.html

Cerbin, B. (2008). [Instructors' responses to *Lesson Study Experience Questionnaire*]. Unpublished raw data.

Cerbin, B. (2009a, March). Assessing how students learn. *Carnegie Perspectives: A Different Way to Think About Teaching and Learning,* Carnegie Foundation for the Advancement of Teaching and Learning. Retrieved from http://www.carnegiefoundation.org/perspectives/assessing-how-students-learn

Cerbin, B. (2009b, October). *What happens when college teachers do lesson study?* Paper presented at the Annual Conference of the International Society for the Scholarship of Teaching and Learning, Bloomington, IN.

Cerbin, B., & Kopp, B. (2003). Lesson study project website. Retrieved from http://www.uwlax.edu/sotl/lsp/

Cerbin, B., Wilson, C., Cary, M., & Dixon, R. (2007, March). A lesson study of bystander intervention: Explaining behavior in terms of multiple variables. *Teaching Forum: A Journal of the Scholarship of Teaching and Learning (Special Issue: Using Lesson Study to Advance Teaching and Learning).* Retrieved from http://www.uwlax.edu/teachingforum/index.html

Cerbin, W., & Kopp, B. (2006). Lesson study as a model for building pedagogical knowledge and improving teaching. *International Journal of Teaching and Learning in Higher Education, 18*(3), 250–257. Retrieved from http://www.isetl.org/ijtlhe/pdf/IJTLHE110.pdf

Chick, N., Hassel, H., Haynie, A., Beck, T., & Kopp, B. (2007, March). Reading for complexity: Recognizing and valuing ambiguity in literature. *Teaching Forum: A Journal of the Scholarship of Teaching and Learning (Special issue: Using Lesson Study to Advance Teaching and Learning).* Retrieved from http://www.uwlax.edu/teachingforum/index.html

Chick, N., Hassel, H., & Haynie, A. (2009). Pressing an ear against the hive: Reading literature for complexity *Pedagogy, 9*(3), 399–422.

Chilton, G., Current, M., Holman, J., Prucha, C., Putz, J., Reinert, T., & Belter, B. (2007, March). Teaching library information literacy skills to students enrolled in an introductory communication course: A collaborative study. *Teaching Forum: A Journal of the Scholarship of Teaching and Learning (Special Issue: Using Lesson Study to Advance Teaching and Learning).* Retrieved from http://www.uwlax.edu/teachingforum/index.html

Clement, J. J. (1982). Students' preconceptions in introductory mechanics. *American Journal of Physics, 50*(1), 66–71.

Dewey, J. (1910). *How we think.* Boston, MA: D. C. Heath.

Ericsson, A., Krampe, R., & Tesch-Romer, C. (1993). The role of deliberate practice in the acquisition of expert performance. *Psychological Review, 100*(3), 363–406.

Fernandez, C., & Yoshida, M. (2004). *Lesson study: A Japanese approach to improving mathematics teaching and learning.* Mahwah, NJ: Lawrence Erlbaum Associates.

Gardner, H. (1991). *The unschooled mind: How children think and how schools should teach.* New York, NY: Basic Books.

Gurung, R., Chick, N., & Haynie, A. (2009). *Exploring signature pedagogies: Approaches to teaching disciplinary habits of mind.* Sterling, VA: Stylus.

Halonen, J. S., Appleby, D. C., Brewer, C. L., Buskist, W., Gillem, A. R., Halpern, D., . . . Whitlow, V. M. (Eds). (2002, March). *Assessment cyberguide for learning goals and outcomes in the undergraduate psychology major.* (Available from the American Psychological Association, http://www.apa.org/ed/governance/bea/assess.aspx?item=5)

Hammerness, K., Darling-Hammond, L., & Shulman, L. (2002). Toward expert thinking: How curriculum case writing prompts the development of theory-based professional knowledge in student teachers. *Teaching Education, 13*(2), 219–243.

Hiebert, J., Gallimore, R., & Stigler, J. (2002). A knowledge base for the teaching profession: What would it look like and how can we get one? *Educational Researcher, 31*(5), 3–15.

Ifill, G. (2007). *Nobel Prize winner for medicine details gene modification work,* Interview with Mario Capeechi. PBS News Hour, Aired October 8, 2007. Retrieved from http://www.pbs.org/newshour/bb/health/july-dec07/nobel_10-08.html

Lewis, C. (Producer). (2000a). *Can you lift 100kg?* [Motion picture]. Japan: Komae School #7.

Lewis, C. (2000b, April). *Lesson study: The core of Japanese professional development.* Paper presented at the Special Interest Group on Research in Mathematics Education at American Educational Research Association meeting, New Orleans, LA.

Lewis, C. (2002a). Does lesson study have a future in the United States? *Nagoya Journal of Education and Human Development, 1,* 1–23.

Lewis, C. (2002b). *Lesson study: A handbook of teacher-led instructional change.* Philadelphia, PA: Research for Better Schools.

Lewis, C. (2005). How do teachers learn during lesson study? In P. Wang-Iverson & M. Yoshida (Eds.), *Building our understanding of lesson study.* Philadelphia, PA: Research for Better Schools.

Lewis, C., Perry, R., & Hurd, J. (2004). A deeper look at lesson study. *Educational Leadership, 61*(5), 18–23.

Lewis, C., Perry, R., Hurd, J., & O'Connell, M. P. (2006). Lesson study comes of age in North America. *Phi Delta Kappan, 88*(4), 273–281.

Lewis, C., Perry, R., & Murata, A. (2004). *What counts as evidence of learning from practice? Collaborative critique of lesson study research methods.* Paper presented at the annual meeting of the American Educational Research Association, San Diego, CA.

Lewis, C., Perry, R., & Murata, A. (2006). How should research contribute to instructional improvement? The case of lesson study. *Educational Researcher, 35*(3), 3–14.

Lewis, C., Takahashi, A., Murata, A., & King, E. (2003). *Developing "the eyes to see students": Data collection during lesson study.* Paper presented at the National Council of Teachers of Mathematics Conference, San Antonio, TX.

Lewis, C., & Tsuchida, I. (1998a). The basics in Japan: The three C's. *Educational Leadership, 55*(6), 32–37.

Lewis, C., & Tsuchida, I. (1998b). A lesson is like a swiftly flowing river. *American Educator, 22*(4), 12–17; 50–52.

Means, B., Toyama, Y., Murphy, R., Bakia, M., & Jones, K. (2009). *Evaluation of evidence-based practices in online learning: A meta-analysis and review of online learning studies.* Center for Technology in Learning. U. S. Department of Education, Office of Planning, Evaluation, and Policy Development, Policy and Program Studies Service. http://www2.ed.gov/rschstat/eval/tech/evidence-based-practices/finalreport.pdf

Meyer, J. H. F., & Land, R. (2003, May). *Threshold concepts and troublesome knowledge: Linkages to ways of thinking and practising.* ETL Project, University of Edinburg, Occasional Report 4.

Nathan, M. J., & Petrosino, A. J. (2003). Expert blind spot among preservice teachers. *American Educational Research Journal, 40*(4), 905–928.

Roback, P., Chance, B., Legler, & Moore, T. (2006). Applying Japanese lesson study principles to an upper-level undergraduate statistics course. *Journal of Statistics Education, 14*(2).

Schwartz, D., & Bransford, J. (1998). A time for telling. *Cognition and Instruction, 16*(4), 475–522.

Shulman, L. (1986). Those who understand: Knowledge growth in teaching. *Educational Researcher, 15*(2), 4–14.

Shulman, L. (1987). Knowledge and teaching: Foundations of the new reform. *Harvard Educational Review, 57*(1), 1–22.

Shulman, L. (1998). Course anatomy: The dissection and analysis of knowledge through teaching. In Pat Hutchings (Ed.), *The course portfolio: How faculty can examine their teaching to advance practice and improve student learning.* Washington, DC: American Association for Higher Education.

Shulman, L. (2002). Making Differences: A Table of Learning. *Change, 34*(6), 36–44.

Shulman, L. (2005). Pedagogies of uncertainty. *Liberal Education, 91*(2), 18–25.

Stigler, J. W., & Hiebert, J. (1999). *The teaching gap: Best ideas from the world's teachers for improving education in the classroom.* New York, NY: Free Press.

Trout, J. D. (2009). *The empathy gap.* New York, NY: Viking.

Tyler, R. (1949). *Basic principles of curriculum and instruction.* Chicago, IL: University of Chicago Press.

Vosniadou, S. (Ed.). (2008). *International handbook of research on conceptual change.* New York, NY: Routledge.

Wang-Iverson, P., & Yoshida, M. (2005). *Building our understanding of lesson study.* Philadelphia, PA: Research for Better Schools.

Wiggins, G., & McTighe, J. (2005). *Understanding by design* (2nd ed.). Alexandria, VA: Association of Supervision and Curriculum Development.

Willingham, D. (2009). *Why don't students like school?* San Francisco, CA: John Wiley.

Wilson, C., Cerbin, W., Cary, M., & Dixon, R. (2007, March). Construct validity in psychological measurement. *Teaching Forum: A Journal of the Scholarship of Teaching and Learning (Special Issue: Using Lesson Study to Advance Teaching and Learning)*. Retrieved from http://www.uwlax.edu/teachingforum/index.html

Wineburg, S. (2001). *Historical thinking and other unnatural acts: Charting the future of teaching the past* (pp. 63–112). Philadelphia, PA: Temple University Press.

Yoshida, M. (1999). *Lesson study: An enthnographic investigation of school-based teacher development in Japan* (Unpublished doctoral dissertation) University of Chicago, Illinois.

Yoshida, M. (2005). An overview of lesson study. In P. Wang-Iverson & M. Yoshida (Eds.), *Building our understanding of lesson study*. Philadelphia, PA: Research for Better Schools.

Index

adaptive expertise, as learning goal, 42–43
analysis, 16–18
  debriefing, 93–95
  difficulties with, 125
  drilling down, 95
  of observational data, 96
  prompts for, 27
  reflection on, 127
  of students' written work, 96–97
audio recordings. *See* recordings

backward design, 12–13, 31, 53–54
  difficulties with, 125
behavior, social, as outcome, 84*t*
behavioral indicators, of learning goals, 35, 36*t*

Capeechi, Mario, 71
cases, lesson plan based on, 52
checklists, 73, 82, 84–85
clinical interview, 82, 87
CLSP. *See* College Lesson Study Project
cognitive domain, learning goals in, 33*t*
cognitive empathy, 13
  designing lesson for, 54–56
collaboration
  in design, 53
  reflection on, 126–27
College Lesson Study Project (CLSP), 8
  approaches to research in, 99–100
  collaboration in, 53
  debriefing in, 95
  and documentation, 103, 106–7
  and learning goals, 33–34

ConcepTests, and student learning, 65
confidence, reflection on, 129
critical thinking, as learning goal, 36–38

data collection, 14–15, 72
  strategies for, 73, 81–87
debriefing, 16–18, 93–95
  prompts for, 26
deliberate practice, 137–38
design
  backward, 12–13, 31, 53–54, 125
  collaborative, 53
  example of, 57–60, 59*t*
  of lesson, 48
  term, 53
Dewey, John, 39
disciplines
  and lesson planning, 49*b*
  teams based on, 20–21
discussion
  lesson plan based on, 51–52
  online, 52, 82
  and student learning, 66
dispositions, as learning goal, 40, 42*t*
documentation/dissemination, 18–19, 101–7
  procedures for, 22
  prompts for, 28–29
  during study, 102*b*
drilling down, 95

educational research
  lesson study and, 99
  misconceptions on, 100*b*

Also available from Stylus

Co-published with the National Teaching and Learning Forum
New Pedagogies and Practices for Teaching in Higher Education series
Editor: James Rhem

Each volume of the series presents a specific pedagogy. The editors and contributors introduce the reader to the underlying theory and methodology, provide specific guidance in applying the pedagogy, and offer case studies of practice across a several disciplines, usually across the domains of the sciences, humanities, and social studies, and, if appropriate, professional studies.

Cooperative Learning in Higher Education
Across the Disciplines, Across the Academy
Edited by Barbara Millis
Foreword by James Rhem

Research has identified cooperative learning as one of the ten High Impact Practices that improve student learning.

Experienced users of cooperative learning demonstrate how they use it in settings as varied as a developmental mathematics course at a community college, and graduate courses in history and the sciences, and how it works in small and large classes, as well as in hybrid and online environments. The authors describe the application of cooperative learning in biology, economics, educational psychology, financial accounting, general chemistry, and literature at remedial, introductory, and graduate levels.

The chapters showcase cooperative learning in action, at the same time introducing the reader to major principles such as individual accountability, positive interdependence, heterogeneous teams, group processing, and social or leadership skills.

Just in Time Teaching
Across the Disciplines, Across the Academy
Edited by Scott Simkins, Mark Maier
Foreword by James Rhem

Just-in-Time Teaching (JiTT) is a pedagogical approach that requires students to answer questions related to an upcoming class a few hours beforehand, using an online course management system. While the phrase "just in time" may evoke shades of slap-dash work and cut corners, JiTT pedagogy is just the opposite. It helps students to view learning as a process that takes time, introspection, and persistence.

Students who experience JiTT come to class better prepared, and report that it helps to focus and organize their out-of-class studying. Their responses to JiTT questions make gaps in their learning visible to the teacher prior to class, enabling him or her to address learning gaps while the material is still fresh in students' minds—hence the label "just in time."

This book demonstrates that JiTT has broad appeal across the academy. Part I provides a broad overview of JiTT, introducing the pedagogy and exploring various dimensions of its use without regard to discipline. Part II of the book demonstrates JiTT's remarkable cross-disciplinary impact with examples of applications in physics, biology, the geosciences, economics, history, and the humanities.

22883 Quicksilver Drive
Sterling, VA 20166-2102

Subscribe to our e-mail alerts: www.Styluspub.com